THE OLD SOUTH
IN THE CRUCIBLE OF WAR

The Old South in the Crucible of War

Essays by
EMORY M. THOMAS
PAUL D. ESCOTT
LAWRENCE N. POWELL
AND MICHAEL S. WAYNE
LEON F. LITWACK
MICHAEL BARTON
THOMAS B. ALEXANDER

Edited by
HARRY P. OWENS
JAMES J. COOKE

UNIVERSITY PRESS OF MISSISSIPPI
Jackson

Copyright © 1983 by the
University Press of Mississippi
All rights reserved
Manufactured in the United States of America

THIS BOOK HAS BEEN SPONSORED
BY THE UNIVERSITY OF MISSISSIPPI

Library of Congress Cataloging in Publication Data
Main entry under title:
The Old South in the crucible of war.

   Papers from the Seventh Annual Chancellor's
Symposium on Southern History, held at the University of
Mississippi, 1981 and sponsored by the Dept. of History,
University of Mississippi.
   Contents: Reckoning with rebels / Emory M. Thomas—
The failure of Confederate nationalism : the Old South's
class system in the crucible of war / Paul D. Escott—
Self-interest and the decline of Confederate
nationalism / Lawrence N. Powell, Michael S. Wayne—
[etc.]
   1. Confederate States of America—History—Congresses.
2. Nationalism—Southern States—History—19th century—
Congresses.   3. United States—History—Civil War,
1861–1865—Congresses.   I. Thomas, Emory M., 1939–
II. Owens, Harry P.   III. Cooke, James J.   IV. Chan-
cellor's Symposium on Southern History (7th : 1981 :
University of Mississippi)   V. University of Mississippi.
Dept. of History.
E487.04   1983   975'.03   83-10361
ISBN 0-87805-191-0
ISBN 0-87805-192-9 (pbk.)

Contents

Preface

The Seventh Annual Chancellor's Symposium held in 1981, at the University of Mississippi, presented a topic which was generated by the provocative scholarship of Professor Emory M. Thomas and other historians who have considered the problem of continuity through the era of the Civil War and Reconstruction. Historians use the Civil War as the dividing line between the Old South and the New South, and such a division implies that the Old South came to an abrupt end. Certainly all historians recognize continuing themes between the Old South and the New. Nevertheless, recent scholarship has demanded a more thorough examination of these lines of persisting themes. The Department of History of the University of Mississippi agreed to raise the question: what happened to the Old South in the crucible of Civil War?

The myths and realities of the Old South evolved through the interplay of frontier conditions, agrarian economics, and Negro slavery. During the four decades preceding the Civil War, the overpowering hegemony of slavery and the plantation economy created a unique section of the United States. Facing mounting criticisms of the "peculiar institution," being outpaced by external economic developments, and threatened by the surging intellectual movements of national growth, the Old South responded by creating an orthodox point of view. Southerners who adhered to the Old South orthodoxy accelerated the process of sectional identity. As the tempo increased during the 1850s, sectionalism was transformed into a nascent nationalism, and nationalism found its time with the Confederacy.

Professor Emory M. Thomas, the foremost historian of Confederate experience, defined the Confederacy as "an extended moment during which Southerners attempted simultaneously to define themselves as a people and to act out a national identity" and he characterized the Confederacy as "the logical extension of ante-bellum Southern ideology." But, during four years in the crucible of war, the South experienced fundamental changes. The Confederate search for national identity required "Southerners [to give up] up, in one way or another, most of those characteristics that called the Confederacy into being."[1] While Professor Thomas interpreted Southern nationalism as costing Southerners *most* of their traditional characteristics, other historians have emphasized the "continuity" and "persistence" of Old South ideology far beyond the Civil War years.

The Department of History invited six prominent historians to present papers at the Seventh Annual Chancellor's Symposium on Southern History. They were asked to examine the South during the four years of the Confederacy and to reflect on the theme of continuity, or lack of it. The symposium directors suggested rather broad topics consistent with the general theme. While the authors were not asked to present footnotes, we are pleased to include those that were submitted.

Professor Emory M. Thomas' theses in his work *The Confederate Nation* (1979) quite naturally set the stage for the 1981 Symposium. Unlike a strawman, he raised additional questions. Was the unique folk culture of the Old South changed in the crucible of war? What happened to the revolutionary changes brought about by Confederacy? Did Confederate defeat bring an end to the nationalizing and modernizing trends of the four war years? Professor Thomas' conclusions spur further study.

The author of *Jefferson Davis and the Failure of Confederate Nationalism* (1979), Paul D Escott, investigated the Old South's class system during the four years of war. Did wartime pressures sharpen the tensions between the planter and yeoman classes? Did the facts of war and defeat reduce the stress and strain between the planter and yeoman classes? Or did defeat bring a greater degree of solidarity to the class structure of the Old South?

Two historians, Lawrence N. Powell and Michael S. Wayne, noted for their interest in the history of the Lower Mississippi River Valley during the era of Civil War and Reconstruction, raised questions of planter loyalty. Planters in the lower Mississippi River Valley were, indeed, in the crucible of war as they faced two opposing armies. Professors Powell and Wayne investigated the course of Confederate nationalism as the planters faced the dilemma of redefining their loyalties. Did self interest or national interest prevail? Did the crucible of war burn the issue to its simplest form: "homestead" or "homeland"?

Four million slaves were also placed in the crucible of war and faced the enormity of the conflict which surrounded them. Professor Leon F. Litwack author of the prize-winning study, *Been in the Storm Too Long* (1980), focused on the sometimes contradictory actions flowing from "traditional" slave responses and the new moods and directions developing among Black Americans as the war raged around them. He poignantly posited the paradox of the ending of slavery and the continuing reality of white supremacy.

Professor Michael Barton brought quantification methodologies to bear on the Confederate soldier. In a delightfully witty essay, he transcended the too often dull repetition of statistics, co-efficients, and correlations to offer a meaningful evaluation of the private and personal attitudes of Southerners serving in the Confederate Armies. Examining letters and diaries of officers and soldiers, Professor Barton asked: were Confederate soldiers' loyalties, identity, and interests reduced to ashes in the crucible of war? Did their identification with the Confederacy survive the losses, reverses, and final defeat on the battlefield? Professor

Barton not only raised questions and provided some answers, he also supplied a list of diaries and letters which he used. These may be found in the end notes.

Professor Thomas B. Alexander, because of his outstanding scholarship and his understanding of the themes of "continuity" and "persistence," was given the most difficult task. He was asked to summarize the problems and the recent scholarship discussing continuity from the Old to the New South. The directors of the symposium even asked him to point to new directions. He admirably fulfilled our request. The questions which he raised, and his suggestions for future research, will keep students of Civil War history active for years.

The Department of History of the University of Mississippi expresses its appreciation to the Mississippi Committee on the Humanities and its director, Dr. Cora Norman, for their support of the 1981 Chancellor's Symposium on Southern History. The Committee's support for this symposium, as their support in previous years, has not only strengthened scholarship but also expanded a concern for the humanities.

The Department of History expresses its indebtedness to Chancellor Porter Lee Fortune for his continuing support. The Center for the Study of Southern Culture contributed time, energy, and valuable suggestions in so many ways, often unrecognized, to make the 1981 Symposium successful. We are grateful for their contributions.

The directors wish to thank all members of the Department of History for their encouragement, help, and support in the Seventh annual Chancellor's Symposium on Southern History.

HARRY P. OWENS
JAMES J. COOKE
University, Mississippi 1982

THE OLD SOUTH
IN THE CRUCIBLE OF WAR

Reckoning With Rebels

EMORY M. THOMAS

The short story "A Late Encounter with the Enemy" is one of Flannery O'Connor's gems. It is about Tennessee Flintrock Sash who is a hundred-and-four-year-old Confederate veteran and his granddaughter. Sally Poker Sash, the granddaughter, was preparing to graduate from a Southern State teachers college at age sixty two, and she wanted her grandfather on the stage when she received her degree. She wanted him there to display "what all was behind her." She would use the old man to say to a tawdry them. "See him! See him! My kin, all you upstarts! Glorious upright old man standing for the traditions! Dignity! Honor! Courage! See him!"

As the story develops the reader discovers that Tennessee Flintrock Sash did not stand for much of anything; he sat down in his wheel chair and did not remember much about his Confederate service. The only experience he cared about was his part in the premiere of a Hollywood film *(Gone with the Wind?)*. A studio publicity man had given him a general's uniform and displayed him with some of the company's stable of starlets in a parade through downtown Atlanta. So the "General's" Confederacy was phony ballyhoo and beautiful "guls." As for history "what happened then wasn't anything to a man living now and he was living now."

In the end the old man dies on the stage of Sally Poker's graduation, and she is too busy being proud to notice. Flannery

O'Connor leaves the corpse and the reader in a long line at the Coca-Cola machine where the nephew assigned to wheel the "General's" chair has stopped for relief from an August graduation exercise in the deep South.

Flannery O'Connor of course told the story much better than I have, and within the thirteen pages which compose "A Late Encounter with the Enemy" are many revelations, considerable humor, and ample irony regarding the human condition. But one of the circumstances which attracts me to this story and moves me to reread it periodically is its preoccupation with the past in general and specifically with the heritage of the late Confederate States of America. Sally Poker and Tennessee Flintrock Sash have problems with the past. The old man was part of the Confederate past but does not remember and never tries to remember; he is preoccupied with "living now." His granddaughter seems intent upon living "then;" she clings to a mythhistory and depends upon it to define and justify her.

Certainly the Sashes are caricatures. But real people seem to have quite as many problems with the Confederate heritage as O'Connor's "freaks." Let me mention some examples.

In autumn of 1978 the United States Congress passed a bill restoring full citizenship upon Jefferson Davis. On signing the bill into law then President Jimmy Carter pronounced, "It is fitting that Jefferson Davis should no longer be singled out for punishment." Because the late President of the Confederacy has been dead for more than ninety years, the actions of Congress and the President were thoroughly symbolic. Tombstones have been known to vote in this country; but it is doubtful that Davis' physical remains, if indeed they remain, will be likely to vote or hold public office. However moot the gesture and mute the subject, I question quite seriously whether the soul, shade, spirit, or whatever of citizen Davis approves of the whole business. Regarding reconciliation, the live Davis wrote to a friend, "It will not be possible for me to join the throng who hurrah for the pillagers and house-burners who invaded our homes." To the

Mississippi legislature he explained that he had never requested a pardon from the government, because repentance must precede pardon, "and I have not repented."

To compound the irony of bestowing citizenship upon a recalcitrant corpse, the President General of the United Daughters of the Confederacy at the time responded to the event with unrestrained glee. "A dream came true when President Carter signed the bill," she wrote. I realize there is a simple explanation; but it does seem slightly strange that the leader of an organization which exists to celebrate four years of desperate war designed to separate from the United States would be now so enthused about reuniting the Confederate President with his old enemies. On the face of it, it appears about as rational as reintering Bobby Sands in Westminster Abby with an honor guard from the IRA whistling "Rule Britannia" while the detachment commander declares, "A dream came true. . . ."

Consider the use and abuse in recent years at Daniel D. Emmett's minstrel show "walk-around" song "Dixie." During the early 1970s at the University of Georgia, the Georgia (nee Dixie) Redcoat Band refrained from playing the tune at football games. Periodically thereafter isolated and organized clamors from all sorts and conditions of people demanded a restoration of "Dixie" to the band's repertoire. Amid one such uproar in 1974, I entered the fray by way of a column I write for the local newspaper. After reviewing the origin of "Dixie" and its adoption by Confederates as an unofficial national anthem, I pointed out that:

> The words of the song and its minstrel show origins are blatant reminders of a stereotypical portrayal of black people as clowns and fools. To be sure the lost cause of the Confederacy involved much more than racial slavery. Yet "Dixie's" association with the Confederacy makes the song a reminder of the slave era, a time to remember, perhaps, but not celebrate, The Book of Exodus does not say, but it is doubtful that Moses led his people out of Pharoh's bondage with a rousing chorus of the Egyptian national anthem. . . . Too many white Southerners still sing "Dixie" to glorify civil wrongs. Too many black South-

erners still associate the song with pain and oppression. Consequently the "Dixie" issue boils down to a question of taste and
a corporate version of what is supposed to be a characteristically Southern virtue, good manners. The song genuinely
offends a sizeable number of people; it need not be played.

There was and still is monstrous irony in the fact that "Glory
Glory to Old Georgia," the University's "fight song," is an upbeat
arrangement of "The Battle Hymn of the Republic." But it did
and does seem more than a little ironic that an historian of the
Confederacy would take a public stand against the playing of
"Dixie."

I could offer many more examples of confusion and contortion
wrought by the Confederate heritage. Too often the Confederate
period in Southern history has been the subject of myth and
madness. Often, too, the Confederacy repels students, scholars,
and laymen who abhor the perverse causes which come wrapped
in Rebel trappings. Willie Morris became something of a folk
hero among liberated Southerners when he wrote *North Toward
Home*. And surely a Confederate residue composed much of the
"great burden," the "terrible weight," and the "old grievance"
Morris shed when he left the South, fled the Southern past, and
attempted self-imposed exile in the "big cave" (New York). Morris was trying to achieve amnesia to separate himself from a
history he associated with heinous wrongs. At the time he wrote
North Toward Home (1967), many Southerners less introspective
and less articulate than Morris were feeling the same estrange-
ment from the Southern past. I suspect many still do.

For the sake of Jefferson Davis, "Dixie," Willie Morris, and the
rest of us, I suggest the time is long overdue for a fresh look at the
old facts of Confederate history. It is past time to ask new questions of the old story; perhaps in the process the Confederacy
may emerge as more than the source of reaction and irrelevance.
Let me contribute a sample of interpretative judgments about
the Confederate past.

The ante bellum South was "different;" Southerners by 1860

had developed a way of life or lifestyle which diverged from the American mainstream. Although subsequent events, secession and war, would seem to confirm the fact of Southern deviation from the American norm, a substantial number of Southern historians have believed otherwise. Clement Eaton, for example, entitled chapter one of his book *The Growth of Southern Civilization* "The Land of the Country Gentlemen," and in it he wrote about the South of the Revolutionary era as a "liberal democracy." Chapter two, however, was about "The Rise of the Cotton Kingdom" and a South which "like the rising industrialism of the North, . . . placed material profits above human rights." For Eaton the "real" South lay in that period of liberal democracy, and the South associated with slavery and treason was an aberration. In *The Growth of Southern Civilization* and elsewhere, Eaton described a South still grounded in characteristically American virtues, but driven to evil and led into folly by a relatively few willful slaveholders. Eaton's analysis was subtle; his conclusions sincere. Like other open-handed, generous-minded Southerners, he attempted to find a South as open-handed and generous-minded as himself. In so doing, though, Eaton and others have dismissed the South's defection from what they perceived to be traditional American values as exceptional and temporary. The "real" South, they imply, has always been a land of country gentlemen in which independent farmers sit at the feet of the "Sage of Monticello."

Like it or not, however, the Old South was "unAmerican," in the sense that its institutions and culture diverged from the mainstream of the nation. By 1860 the Southern "way of life" involved racial slavery, landed aristocracy, agrarianism, individualism, state rights, romanticism, folk culture and much more. However combined and however precisely defined, these common elements of Southern life became sanctified in the Southern mind and spirit. By way of a process I can best term "secular transsubstantiation," i.e. the transformation of ordinary things into sacred items, Southern lifestyle generated a Southern ideology. This ideology—or belief system or world view or perception of reality—was, like most ideologies, janus-faced; it was the sum, not only of hopes and dreams, but also of fears and threats. And the source of most of those fears and threats was "the Yankee," who possessed a very different ideology.

Primarily, though not exclusively, because of the external threat posed by the North, Southerners chose to leave the Union in 1860–61. Secession was a radical act and in the vanguard of the secession movement was a cadre of so-called "fire-eaters." These people worked long and hard at the tactics of revolution, and at the transit of Southern sectionalism into Southern nationalism. No less than Sam Adams and Patrick Henry did men such as Edmund Ruffin, William Lowndes Yancey, and Robert Barnwell Rhett pursue a radical cause with constancy and success. Thus the attempt to conserve the Southern "way of life" came about when it did, as it did, because of the actions of radicals. And compounding this irony is the fact that the secessionist radicals, having brought the Southern revolution into being, then lost control of it. The fire-eaters occupied little or no prominent place in the Confederacy.

The nation framed and formed at Montgomery was the poltical expression of the Old South status quo. The practical, moderate leadership which asserted itself in the "morning after" aftermath of secession sought no new worlds; they and most of their fellow Southerners were well satisfied with the world that was. Consequently the Confederate founding fathers adopted a constitution which much resembled that of the "old" Union and formed a government whose *summum bonum* was the survival of the status quo. Jefferson Davis probably said it best. In his inaugural address as provisional President, Davis asserted "the right of the people to alter or abolish governments whenever they become destructive of the ends for which they were established." Southerners, he insisted had, "asserted a right which the Declaration of Independence of 1776 had defined to be inalienable." Then having invoked the heritage of 1776 to justify revolution in 1861,

David claimed, "It is by abuse of language that their act [forming the Confederacy] has been denominated a revolution." Within the context of the moment, Davis made sense when he claimed the right of revolution and then claimed that no revolution had taken place. Southerners had employed radical means to achieve conservative ends.

The Confederacy as Old South embalmed reached its zenith on July 21, 1861, on the slopes of Henry House Hill near the town of Manassas and slightly south of a stream called Bull Run. Around four o'clock that afternoon, the see-saw battle which was the first full-scale engagement of the war took a Southern turn. The Federal battle line broke and Union troops streamed to the rear in confusion. To this point the Southern nation was almost precisely what it had been called to be, a celebration of the ante bellum status quo. And at Manassas on that July afternoon the Old South as nation seemed everywhere victorious.

During subsequent months, however, the Confederacy suffered a series of reverses so serious as to confound the spirit of her most steadfast supporters. When Jefferson Davis took the oath of office as permanent President on February 22, 1862, he pronounced the time to be "the darkest hour of our struggle." And the times got still worse. In response to the desparate challenge posed by what became "total" war for national survival, Confederate Southerners made fundamental alterations in the institutions and ideas they had gone to war to protect. Let me now offer a much-abbreviated recitation of some of the alterations wrought by the Confederate experience.

Politically the David administration sacrificed the very doctrine on which the Confederacy was founded—state rights. Although limited by inertia and bureaucratic inefficiency and opposed by some state governors and more tradition-bound politicians and editors, the Richmond government was characterized by centralization and nationalism. The conscription of troops and labor, suspension of the writ of habeas corpus, governmental control of manufacturing, railroads, and vital raw materials, impressment of goods, fixing of consumer prices, and ultimately state socialism were but some of the manifestations of Confederate nationalism. These things and more the Davis government attempted with varying degrees of success for the sake of independence.

Economically, the nation founded by planters to preserve plantation agrarianism became, within the limits of its ability, urbanized and industrialized. Southern cities swelled in size and importance. Richmond more than doubled in population; Atlanta was born; and Selma, Alabama became a center of war industry. With the aid of government contracts and assistance, Southern industry made remarkable strides. Cotton, sacrosanct as "king" before the war, became a veritable "pawn" in the government's control of foreign trade, in the conduct of diplomacy, and in the accumulation of capital for war industries. The Confederacy's emphasis on manufacturing and urbanization came too little and too late. But compared to the ante bellum South, the Confederate South underwent nothing short of an economic revolution.

There was social revolution, too. Southerners had thought they were a stable people, but the Confederacy and its war changed their minds. Whatever else it did, the Confederate era brought varieties of experience hitherto unknown below the Potomac. Food riots plagued Southern cities. An incipient Southern proletariat exhibited a marked degree of class awareness. Southern "belles" climbed down from their pedestals and went to work in factories and domestic industries or assumed responsibility for running farms. Military and governmental service created new avenues to social status and to some extent democratized Southern social mores. And the war made Confederates put away many of their self-delusions. To admit that one Southerner could not whip ten Yankees was at least a step away from romanticism toward reality.

By 1864 under the pressure of war the Confederate South had surrendered much of its cherished "way of life." In contrast to the ante bellum status quo, the Confederacy became characterized by tendencies toward political nationalism, industrialism, urbanization, realism, an aristocracy of merit, national culture, and liberated womanhood. However in 1865 there still remained one final sacred cow to be sacrificed on the altar of independence.

If the Southern "way of life" contained one *sine qua non*, that essential ingredient was slavery. The Confederacy "used" free and bonded blacks in many ways unknown in the ante bellum South. Despite this, slavery in the Confederate South has been described by Bell Wiley as a "dying institution." Then during the fall and winter of 1864 Confederates engaged in a national debate over no less an issue than emancipation of Southern slaves. The process began in earnest in November when Jefferson Davis proposed to acquire 40,000 slaves for noncombatant military duties and to free them upon completion of faithful service. Rapidly this "radical modification," as Davis phrased it, broadened to include a proposal to recruit black troops for Confederate armies. Discussion centered upon whether or not to arm the slaves; but at base the question was freedom for Southern blacks. Georgian Howell Cobb, who opposed the use of black troops, best expressed the root issue. "The day you make soldiers of them," Cobb stated, "is the beginning of the end of the revolution. If slaves will make good soldiers our whole theory of slavery is wrong." Eventually, after much hue and cry from politicians and the press, the Confederate Congress authorized recruitment of 200,000 black soldiers. The Congress shrank from authorizing "a change in the relation which the said slaves shall bear toward their owners." But common sense dictated that men who had served their country as soldiers could never again be its chattels. And to make sure of this, the Confederate War Office refused to accept slaves into the army; every black Confederate soldier was to have "the rights of a freedman."

By the time the Confederacy organized the first company of black troops, the end was very near. The evacuation of Richmond and surrender at Appomattox ended Jefferson Davis' pretensions to becoming "the great emancipator." Nevertheless Confederate

Southerners had confronted the issue and shown themselves willing to destroy what Vice President Alexander H. Stephens in 1861 had termed their "cornerstone." Davis, Robert E. Lee, and others embraced the "radical modification" in the hope of preserving Southern independence.

The interpretation of the Confederate experience as a transformation of the ante bellum South sketched above is of course open to serious question. At numerous points the issue might best be compared to an eight ounce glass containing four ounces of liquid. Many historians have and will observe that the glass is half-empty—that the Confederacy confronted its archaic institutions only in desperation and usually too late. I see the glass half-full; I am impressed that the confrontations occurred at all. But given these questions, the above analysis all but demands answers to three more questions. Therefore let me conclude by asking these three questions and attempting a brief response to each.

First, if Confederate Southerners were willing to sacrifice so much of what had once defined them as a people, for what did they fight and sacrifice during the grim campaigns of late 1864 and 1865? As the editor of the Jackson *News* phrased it in the heat of debate over emancipation, "Why fight one moment longer, if the object and occasion of the fight is dying, dead, or damned?" I suggest that by this time the Confederacy had become for many Southerners an end in itself. The war experience had molded Southerners and defined them as a people. Hence they continued a struggle for what Woodrow Wilson would later term "self-determination of peoples." And there was in fact at least one distinctive Southern trait which Confederate Southerners showed themselves unwilling to sacrifice for the sake of prolonging the war. Historian David Potter once suggested that a unique folk culture—a primacy of personal relationships and attachments to place—lay at the base of Southern identity. Confederate Southerners surely affirmed the persistence of folk culture when in 1865 they all but unanimously rejected the option of guerrilla warfare. The option was viable and no less a person than Jefferson Davis, not only counseled, but ordered it. Nevertheless the Confederates refused to become partisans and their refusal, it seems to me, is significant. Guerrilla war demanded that soldiers abandon family and friends and become nomads. The Confederates would have none of it.

The second question involves the permanence, or lack of it, of those changes wrought by the Confederate experience. What happened to nationalism, industrialization and the rest during the post-war years? I suggest that many of the positive or "modern" aspects of the Confederate experience did not survive the total defeat and destruction of the Confederate state. And Reconstruction, not only failed to enforce the war aims of the Union, but also served to frustrate the positive elements of the Confederate experience. From this defeat and these frustrations the "New South" emerged. Yet nothing is so striking about the New South as its resemblance to the Old South. If the Confederacy was a classic revolutionary experience for Southerners, then the New South was the "Thermidor," the conservative reaction.

Finally, the third question is simply, So what? What does all this mean and how can the Confederate past enlighten the Southern present?

All people it seems to me, live in a tension between past and present and face the challenge of acting out of past experience in an ever novel present, of living with the past but in the present. This tension though, seems especially acute for modern Southerners. For as novelist Walker Percy projects:

> The likeliest future of the region is an ever more prosperous Southern Rim stretching from coast to coast, Los Angeles— Dallas—Atlanta—axis, and the agribusiness, sports, vacation, retirement, showbiz culture with its spiritual center perhaps at Oral Roberts University; its media center in Atlanta, its entertainment industry shared by Disney World, the Super Dome and Hollywood.

In the midst of such a circumstance Southerners will be, as all

people are, products of their experience. I suggest that a renewed understanding of the creative aspects of the Confederate
experience would amply reward the effort.

The Failure of Confederate Nationalism: The Old South's Class System in the Crucible of War

PAUL D. ESCOTT

The Old South was not old. In 1860 it was still a youthful, developing society rather than a venerable civilization. Only two generations before secession, the land west of the Appalachians had been occupied by the Indians; little more than one hundred years had passed since families moved into piedmont portions of the seaboard states; and outside of Virginia and Charleston there were few areas that had significant roots in the seventeeth century.

The Civil War created the Old South in the sense that it thrust this society into the past. By ending slavery, the war established a demarkation and made the slave South a part of history. But in terms of the society that had been developing, this nomenclature was artificial. The South had grown rapidly, stimulated by the boom of short-staple cotton. It had begun to exhibit its own distinct character, but in 1860 the society had reached something akin to late adolescence rather than old age. The Civil War can be thought of as a furious rite of passage—a severe test that forced the society to confront its weaknesses if it was to attain the maturity of nationhood.

"A severe test or trial" is one meaning of crucible, and the Confederate experience certainly satisfies that definition.[1] Crucible also means a refractory vessel used over fire to melt ores; in this sense I would suggest that the war generated fires of unprecedented intensity, and the government of Jefferson Davis became the refractory vessel that contained the heat of these fires and directed it inward upon the mettle of the Old South. As a crucible's heat melts iron, so the stresses of war melted the rigid amalgam called the Old South, revealing the elements from which it was made. In the crucible of Confederate experience, the essential qualities and contradictions of the Old South bubbled to the surface.

Crucible suggests still a further meaning, a transformation of some kind. In industrial processes the heat and fire produce a change within the vessel—the ore is refined, the metal purified, or a new substance is created. Something different emerges from the crucible. Can this be said of the Confederacy?

I think not. Despite enormous changes, the molten elements of southern society did not bond together to form a new and stronger alloy. The imperious demands of war and the determined policies of the Davis administration kept the Confederacy fighting, but an inspiring sense of nationalism did not emerge to give purpose to the effort. The Old South could not transform itself as the crisis required.

Instead, I shall urge, the needs of the Confederacy collided with fundamental and intransigent aspects of the Southern class system. Confederate nationalism failed in large part, of course, because it encountered the massive superiority of northern resources and the demoralizing effects of defeat. But it also foundered upon the tensions and contradictions of a class system that could not sustain both aristocracy and democracy during a severe crisis. It suffered from the profound misjudgment and narrow vision of a leadership class that proved unqualified to lead. The war revealed basic flaws in the social system that political leaders of the antebellum South had loudly praised.

But, ironically, defeat confirmed essential features of the Old South instead of discrediting them. For basic elements of the class system, the caste system, and a sense of regional identity survived to exert a continuing influence on Southern history.

As Emory Thomas has shown, the Confederacy was a period of

immense change for the South, a "revolutionary experience."[2] During the brief life of the Confederacy, the lives of the Southern people changed with startling rapidity and thoroughness. Fundamental aspects of society were challenged. The Confederate experience deserves to be taken seriously on its own terms, neither dismissed as an aberration nor treated as a reflection of other periods.

Before the war, the Old South was known for its agrarian way of life and its reliance upon Negro slaves to produce cotton and other market crops. The Old South's politics had been distinguished by an aggressive devotion to state rights, and its social values had been marked by the aristocratic pretensions of the elite and by more widely shared values such as individualism, romanticism, and localism.

The Civil War changed every one of these areas of distinctiveness. Survival required a strong new emphasis on industry and on food crops rather than cotton. Necessity dictated the rapid growth of a large and powerful central government—an unprecedented development, whether or not it was compatible with state-rights constitutionalism. The logic of events encouraged promotion by merit, collective consciousness, and sacrifice of individual independence for the common good.

Though they took place in a brief period, all these changes were real. The Richmond administration, with its extensive bureaucracy, became the engine that drove the war effort forward. Factories grew and cities expanded as the social environment was transformed. For many Southerners attitudes changed quickly because the world had changed radically. Some Confederates requested the Richmond administration to impose price controls, even martial law, as a way of controlling inflation and extortion. Thousands of yeoman families surrendered their fierce independence to seek relief from poverty. Ultimately the Davis government proved willing to sacrifice slavery itself in pursuit of independence.[3]

But the meaning of these changes lies in how people felt about them, and here I depart from Emory Thomas. If I read him correctly, he suggests that the crucible of the Confederacy changed the Old South; it created the Confederate Nation, even though that nation met defeat. Though my scholarly debt to Professor Thomas is very large, I evaluate the Confederate experience in different terms from his. Perhaps this is a matter of personality—as he has put it, some people say that an eight-ounce glass containing four ounces of water if half-full, others say half-empty. But I think an important historical point is at issue.

I believe that—for Southerners—the Confederacy was an unwelcome experience, a change that the majority of Southerners came to oppose. A spirit of Confederate nationalism failed to develop, and voluntary support for the war effort progressively disintegrated. The roots of this failure lay in the Southern class system as it responded to the stresses of war. The nation did not cohere; and the Old South was not fundamentally changed. It retained a class system based on contradiction and a regional identity that was inescapable, even though it was insufficient to constitute a nation-state.[4]

On the eve of the Civil War the South had attained a regional identity, a sense of itself as a place and as a distinct social system. The creation of the Confederacy, however, was an assertion of something more, a declaration of a sense of nationalism that was not yet present. In 1860 most southerners felt they belonged to the American nation. Some new bond, some sense of Confederate purpose was required to efface those loyalties and establish a Confederate identity. Moreover, in terms of the harsh realities of war, a sense of Confederate nationalism *had* to grow and inspire southerners if they were to emerge from their ordeal as an independent nation.

The responsibility for fostering commitment to the nation fell to Jefferson Davis, who, as a determined but distant personality, was both well and poorly qualified for the task. Davis devoted himself irrevocably to Confederate independence, and intially he nurtured the frail spirit of nationalism with skill. He organized a government and articulated an ideology that avoided potential disagreements. By emphasizing that the Confederacy was the embodiment and continuation of American political principles, his ideology invited the many southerners who still had affection for the United States to transfer their loyalty to the new government. Collisions with Northern armies stimulated an outpouring of regional loyalty for the sake of self-defense. In the late summer of 1861 Southern unity was at its zenith, and the prospects for growth of a national spirit seemed bright.[5]

By early 1862, however, "the spirit of volunteering had died out," and serious problems multiplied thereafter—long before the military situation became hopeless. The next year, 1863, brought further deterioration and calamities that put the growth of disaffection beyond the government's control; by 1864 the Davis administration was struggling against disintegration.[6] What had happened? The sources of these ills provide a clue to their cause.

The Confederacy's internal problems appeared at the top and bottom levels of white society—at the extremes of the class system. The centralizing efforts of the Davis administration offended prominent state rightists, who began a continuing attack on the policies, and even legitimacy, of their own government. Opposition from planters grew as the Richmond government impressed slaves and interfered with plantation routines. Meanwhile poverty invaded the homes of ordinary Southerners who had reason to wonder whether they had as much at stake as the wealthy planters. Worse, Congress' unpopular conscription law discriminated against the poor by giving exemptions to those who managed twenty or more slaves, and the stringent tax-in-kind added to the burdens of an "unequal and odious" impressment law.

In the face of such troubles, Davis' ideology degenerated into little more than racial scare tactics, a desperate effort (often repeated in Southern history) to force white Southerners to pull together out of fear. During 1864 a lack of consensus over war

aims and widespread reluctance to continue the war were pain-
fully evident. Despite the absence of a two-party system, which
tarnished those who proposed alternate policies with the taint of
treason, a variety of peace movements appeared. Long before
the end of the war (in 1863 or certainly in 1864) most Confederates knew the feeling voiced by one bitter farmer: "The sooner
this damned Government [falls] to pieces the better it [will] be
for us."[7]

The failure of Confederate nationalism is apparent in this se-
quence of events and has been documented in various ways.
Thomas Alexander and Richard Beringer have shown that Congress' spirit was marked by a declining willingness to sacrifice,
rather than by revolutionary zeal. They confirmed, as well, Buck
Yearns' finding that as opposition grew the Davis administration
relied more and more heavily on the votes of congressmen whose
districts lay in enemy hands. Popular governors like North
Carolina's Zeb Vance and Georgia's Joe Brown won people's loyalty by expressing the dissatisfactions of poor and rich alike and
by shielding all their citizens, as far as they were able, from the
Confederacy's relentless demands for sacrifice. Successful politics became the art of playing on dissatisfactions without offering
a solution. Politicians who sought solutions by making the hard
choices necessary for survival became unpopular, while those
who denounced stern but necessary policies of the Confederacy
won gratitude and devotion.[8]

The Confederacy did not fall apart. Some ardent secessionists—like Robert B. Rhett of the Charleston *Mercury*—
swallowed their hatred of Davis to support his insistence on independence.[9] Many Southerners endured their dislike of the
Confederacy because their dislike of Yankees was growing even
more rapidly. Because the army rounded up deserters and the
bureaucracy enforced war measures, because Jefferson Davis was
unbending and many soldiers were gritty and courageous, the
South doggedly stayed in the fight until Appomattox. But no

sense of unity or purpose had emerged to turn southern society into a nation.

This failure of Confederate nationalism was inseparably linked to the class system of the Old South. Wartime pressures sharpened the conflicts and contradictions within the social system. The individualism and belief in equality of yeomen Southerners collided with the aristocratic haughtiness and demands for privilege of the planters. Not surprisingly, a slaveowners' government lost the support of nonslaveowners. What is more surprising is that the Confederacy lost the support of many large slaveowners as well. This development was the result of initial misjudgment and subsequent inflexibility on the part of the planter class itself.

The class system of the Old South had sustained an important ambiguity. Among white Southerners, aristocracy had coexisted with democracy. The slaveowners, and planters especially, viewed themselves as a superior, aristocratic class. They savored the power and prestige that derived from ownership of the most valuable form of property in the South: black human beings. Controlling between 90 and 95 percent of the region's agricultural wealth, slaveowners also monopolized most political offices.[10] To them, this was as it should be, for they believed that they were better than the yeomen and were entitled to special influence and privileges.

Despite the inequality that existed in Southern society, yeomen farmers held firmly to a democratic creed. Their outlook was rooted in the frontier experience which tested men for what they were, not what they owned. Yeomen cherished independence, self-reliance, and individualism—values that were supported well into the nineteenth century by the semideveloped, sparsely settled nature of much of the South. They were aware of the planters' pretensions and power, but they did not accept them. The South's political system was formally democratic, thoroughly so in most states, and the yeomen insisted on their rights. Travelers and diarists agreed that the yeomen demanded

social respect as well, often treating planters as equals and requiring gestures of respect from wealthy office seekers.[11]

How could these two opposed value systems coexist in southern society? An answer commonly given is that racism provided
the glue to hold white society together. Generations of politicians
had maintained that enslavement of Afro-Americans made all
white men equal. John C. Calhoun declared, "with us, the two
great divisions of society are not the rich and poor, but white and
black; and all the former, the poor as well as the rich, belong to
the upper classes, and are respected and treated as equals." Jefferson Davis similarly argued that, contrary to all other societies
in which "the line has been drawn, by property, between the rich
and the poor," the southern system allowed nonslaveholders to
"*stand upon the broad level of equality with the rich man.*"[12]

This ideology of "Herrenvolk Democracy," as George Fredrickson has called it, was important and helped to limit class
conflict among whites. I also accept the idea that kinship ties
among planters and nonslaveholders may have assuaged conflict,
and the willingness of wealthy office seekers to compliment the
yeomen and flatter their egos and self-image certainly helped to
lubricate the social system.[13]

Two additional factors, however, were extremely important.
First, as W. J. Cash contended and as Gavin Wright has recently
demonstrated, the yeomen farmers of the South enjoyed economic independence. They were not dependent upon the planters; their attitude of proud self-reliance was rooted in reality.
Relatively few yeomen derived their substance from raising and
driving livestock for the planters, and slaveowners were not dependent on the yeomen. Although heavy planting of cotton was
too risky for most nonslaveholders and the proportion of
slaveowning families was falling, the average wealth of nonslaveholders was increasing. The great majority owned their own
land and had few direct economic relations with planters, who
had their slaves cultivate corn and provisions along with cotton.
Southern wealthholding was unequal (and was becoming more so

because the wealth of slaveholders grew at a faster rate than the wealth of yeomen), but the yeomen were self-sufficient and had reason to feel satisfaction in their own accomplishments.[14]

Second, the very low population density of the South and the localized, rural pattern of life mitigated class tensions. In 1860 the South had the lowest population density of any non-frontier portion of the United States. There were, for example, only 2.3 persons per square mile in Texas, 15.6 in Louisiana, and 18.0 in Georgia. The states that joined the Confederacy averaged only 11.5 persons per square mile; the figure for nonslaveholding states east of the Mississippi River was three times higher, and a state like Massachusetts had 153.1 persons per square mile. Moreover, southerners, though they migrated, generally stayed close to any home they established. Working their farms, they participated in few social organizations beyond family and church. Thus social classes, as collective competing objects, were rarely visible. Where there is little class contact, little class conflict is likely.[15]

The southern economy and social system allowed individuals to pursue their own interests. For yeoman and planter alike there was abundant land, and many southerners moved about during their lives in search of more fertile soil. Geographically and economically the South was expanding. The appetite of British textile mills allowed cotton planters to pursue riches, and nonslaveowners too could aspire to slave-based wealth. Probably many yeomen, however, enjoyed self-sufficiency and shared the view of a Mississippi yeoman, Ferdinand Steel, who concluded, "we are to [sic] weak handed [to grow cotton]. We had better raise small grain and corn and let cotton alone, raise corn and keep out of debt and we will have no necessity of raising cotton." Like Steel, who educated himself and became a Methodist minister, many yeomen dedicated themselves to religion, family and kinship relations, or other interests besides wealth from cotton.[16]

Despite a diversity of motives and outlook, the region possessed some common values. The closeness of the frontier produced attitudes and personality traits held by southerners, high and low. Planters and yeomen alike valued masculine virtues: independence, self-reliance, physical strength, courage, endurance, and personal honor. They lived lives close to nature and enjoyed outdoor sports such as hunting, horseracing, or cock fighting. For planters and yeomen alike individualism was a strong (even fiercely asserted) trait for which society furnished room for expression. It was shared, along with racism and independence.

Thus, the expanding, rural, semi-developed South permitted opposed value-systems to coexist and gave scope for a variety of self-interests. Men could assert themselves and pursue their goals relatively unhindered. They lived very independent lives, and southern society did not require much internal unity or cooperation. At the same time it created the emotional basis for pulling together against outside threats.[17] White southerners felt their unity in certain regional traits, but they had not been forced to confront their differences.

The Civil War forced this confrontation because it demanded heavy sacrifices and radically affected the lives of humbler citizens. As hundreds of thousands of yeomen sank rapidly into poverty, class tensions flared. The proud individualism and democratic outlook of the yeomen stirred them to demand justice (in no uncertain terms). Why was it, asked even a supporter of the government, that "nine tenths of the youngsters of the land whose relatives are conspicuous in society, wealthy, or influential obtain some safe perch where they can doze with their heads under their wings?" A Georgian denounced the "notorious fact [that] if a man has influential friends—or a little money to spare he will never be enrolled." The yeomen believed, as a hill-country newspaper put it, that, "*All classes of the community* MUST *do their share of the fighting*, the high, the low, the rich and poor, and those who have *the means* MUST *pay the* expense. . . ." Hundreds of letters to the War Department echoed this warning: "the people will not *always* submit to this *unequal, unjust* and partial distribution of favor. . . ."[18]

In reponse to these angry protests the aristocrats of the South too often answered with assertive individualism of their own. Consider these phenomena: Robert Toomb's defiant refusal to grow less cotton, the wealthy men who "spent a fortune in substitutes," Congress' refusal to end substitution until the start of 1864, and the arrogant opinion of the *Richmond Examiner* that "this ability to pay [for a substitute] is, in most cases, the best proof of the citizen's social and industrial value." Planters continued to expect privileged treatment, as shown by men like North Carolina's Patrick Edmondston who declined to serve unless given a high command and by the fact that in September, 1864, when the army was desperately short of mules and horses, the War Department was lending them to prominent citizens.[19]

Such self-serving, callous acts by the elite were a slap in the face to the yeomen, and they responded with quiet rebellion. Men who saw themselves as "we poor soldiers who are fighting for the 'rich mans [N]egro'" stopped fighting. Wives urged husbands to "desert again. . . . come back to your wife and children." With calm determination and self-assurance in their course, "many deserters . . . just pat[ted] their guns and . . . sa[id], 'This is my furlough.'" Thousands of others refused to cooperate with tax collectors, enrollment officers and other officials or went into open opposition.[20]

As for the slaveowners, they too had a frustrating and bitter experience, but one they had brought on themselves. For as political leaders they had made a profound mistake. They had launched a revolution to secure conservative ends, and they found that their means and ends were incompatible. To keep their lives and plantations unchanged, they had plunged into a vortex of change. The gamble that secession might be peaceful or war brief was lost, and with it went any hope of attaining their goal amid total war.

To this fact they could not, as a class, adjust. Reality required strong measures, changes of many kinds. Jefferson Davis understood the situation and inaugurated change, but the planter class was frozen in the past and inflexible. As Davis responded to reality, his unpopularity with slaveowners grew. They had used the shibboleth of state rights so often, and resisted central power so long, that they fought against their own government and opposed measures necessary for survival. Their capacity for creative statesmanship had withered, and they ended the war hostile and uncooperative prisoners of their own initiative.[21]

Moreover, the planter class failed to offer a vision for the society it wished to lead and the nation it attempted to create. The planters had no unifying goal in mind and little inclination to seek one; they merely wanted to be left undisturbed in their way of life, their privileges, and their possession of slaves. When the debate over Confederate emancipation occurred, the response of slaveowners was overwhelmingly negative. Thus, they revealed that they valued slavery above independence and had led their society into a cataclysm for nothing beyond a selfish reason: to safeguard their class interests.

The war years witnessed different classes of the white South asserting their interests and resisting the changes thrust upon them. Defeat confirmed this pattern. As many studies have shown, the former slaveowners resisted emancipation vehemently and tenaciously. There were individual exceptions, but in general former slaveowners sought to retain the advantages slavery had given them and offset the decline in their social power. They clung as well to their political principles and continued fighting for state rights, limited government, and a localism that defied conditions the victorious North attempted to impose on the South.[22]

Similarly, yeomen tried to avert the decline in their social position that emancipation threatened. In a racist society their status had benefited from the fact that they were above the caste line. The principle of legal equality promised to erase that distinction. Many yeomen voted Republican, but as many and soon more probably voted Democratic. Historians have established, too, that small farmers were present along with large landowners beneath the robes of the Ku Klux Klan.[23]

This was not surprising, since racism had always been one of the bonds uniting white southerners. After the lack of cohesion apparent in the war years, southerners who desired unity were likely to seek it in the basic elements of agreement. I wonder, however, whether the resurgence of racial oppression and inter-class unity among whites necessarily had to occur so quickly and completely. In the Confederacy class tensions frequently out-weighed shared racial antipathies. If Andrew Johnson had vigor-ously continued in the earlier course of his career, as a champion of the yeomen and foe of the planter, class conflict among whites might have been more visible during Reconstruction and racial unity less prominent. But Johnson's support for the planters late in 1865 removed this possibility. As events subsequently de-veloped, the conversion from class antagonist to racial ally could be thorough. A baffled supporter of North Carolina's William Woods Holden wrote the beleaguered governor in 1870: "I know a great many men who laid out during the war, who were whipped, kicked, and handcuffed by the rebels during the war, who are now among the Ku-Klux, and voted for the men that abused them so badly."[24]

My final point is an obvious, but nonetheless important one. The bloody contests with Yankees had intensified southerners' sense of regional identity. The defeat of the Confederacy and the long intersectional conflict over Reconstruction solidified a dis-tinct and separate image for the South. In later years political use of the bloody shirt by Republicans continued to encourage north-ern hostility toward the South and provoke angry self-consciousness among southerners. Though the New South move-ment insisted that rational lessons should be drawn from defeat, promoters of the Lost Cause ultimately used emotions of loss, hurt, and pride to impose a myth of wartime unity. Moreover, the facts could not be erased: the South was the region that had risked secession, had paid a high price, and had been defeated. Ironically, as time passed the war that had generated tumultuous change became for the region a symbol of continuity.

Self-Interest and the Decline of Confederate Nationalism

LAWRENCE N. POWELL AND
MICHAEL S. WAYNE

Some years ago, in a famous essay entitled "The Historian's Use of Nationalism and Vice Versa," the late David Potter reminded us of some important features of modern nationalism.[1] One of these features is the psychological nature of national loyalty itself, which is but a form of group feeling that differs from most other forms of group feeling only in being more abstract. Subjective in nature, nationalism is thus a relative and not an absolute condition, a dynamic and not a static force, and ebbs and flows according to contingencies. Another signal feature of nationalism, Potter observed, is its compatibility with other kinds of loyalties. Indeed, far from obliterating concrete forms of allegiance—such as attachments to family, property, community, class, and region—nationalistic loyalty subsumes and derives strength from these more immediate allegiances, which in many respects are primary. Finally, Potter stressed a third feature of nationalism that is helpful to bear in mind. This is the fact that nationalism rests on two bases not one: a shared sense of culture *and* a shared set of interests. Historians are extremely apt to emphasize the former and to hypothesize a separate cultural nationalism whenever they detect deep cleavages in a society. But Potter believed, and correctly so, that we should never overlook the component of self-interest to patriotism. As he himself put it, "It is axiomatic that people tend to give their loyalty to institutions which 'protect' them—that is, safeguard their interests—and political loyalty throughout history has been regarded as something given reciprocally in return for protection."[2]

Potter himself was principally concerned with the *formation* of Confederate nationalism. But it is evident his thesis has application to the *disintegration* of the same movement as well. For if self-interest can help explain why people choose to give their allegiance to a particular state, it can also help explain why they might withdraw that allegiance at some point in time.

These thoughts are useful to keep in mind when interpreting the behavior of the planting elite of the lower Mississippi Valley during the two years of wartime occupation. This does not appear to have been their finest hour. Many of them socialized with the enemy, reaped substantial benefits from the illicit cotton trade, and pledged their loyalty now to one side, now the other, as personal advantage seemed to dictate. Selfishness appears to have been their dominant trait, self-interest their only creed. Yet this pattern of wartime behavior reflects something much more basic and profound: the realignment of the planters's political allegiances due to changes in their perceived self-interest; or, to be more accurate, the detachment of that perceived self-interest from *all* sense of national loyalty. Two factors influenced this development. The first was the growing inability of the Richmond government to protect the welfare of the vast majority of its citizens in the Mississippi Valley. The second—and this is an aspect to the story not fully appreciated—was the growing readiness of the Washington government to appease the planters so as to convince them that their material interests would be best served by transferring their allegiances back to the Union.

All this could not have been predicted at the outset of the war. As a general thing, the great planters in the lower Mississippi Valley joined the Confederacy in good faith and with every intention of working for its ultimate success. To be sure, they were not generally committed to secession in the ante bellum period and for the most part disdained the impetuosity of their fire-eating fellow countrymen. Yet when forced to make a choice, they put initial misgivings behind them and went with their section and their state. Lincoln's call for troops after the firing on Fort Sumter was compelling evidence for the secessionists' argument that the security of the slave system and the continuance of planter dominance necessitated forming a new national government. Here was the self-interested component of Confederate nationalism, which in this historical instance probably bulked larger than the cultural component.

Moreover, although they came late to secessionism, they did not come to it with feet dragging. They became ardent on behalf of the cause. A notion has grown up that a significant element of influential slaveholders along the Mississippi remained devoted to the Union throughout the war. But this was a myth created by the planters themselves after the fact and sustained by Northern officials for purposes of their own. Take the case of Stephen Duncan, reputedly at one time the largest single producer of cotton in America, with plantations scattered up and down both sides of the Mississippi. In July, 1863, a federal recruiting party carried off all of the blacks on one of his estates in Louisiana. Duncan obtained their release after securing the personal intervention of General Ulysses S. Grant. "The Duncan's [sic] have been loyal from the beginning of the rebellion," wrote Grant to the officer in charge of the case, "and as loyal persons have had safe guard given them by myself and Admiral Porter." But Grant was in error. Duncan was no patriot, as even a superficial investigation of his past would surely have shown. In September, 1861, he had written a close associate in Kingston, Mississippi, "I have striven hard to satisfy my *former* friends in the North that to force us back, into the union—or to subjugate us—was as impossible as to bale the ocean dry with a bushel basket . . . I still think & *ever shall* think, it *could* have been & *should* have been avoided: but at the same time, I think . . . feel, & know, that it is the duty of every Southron, to unite in the vigorous prosecution of the War." Subsequently Duncan's son went off to enlist in the rebel army and Duncan himself contributed almost 100 slaves to work on the defenses at Vicksburg and Fort Pillow. Even when he moved north in late 1863, months after being rewarded by Grant for his loyalty, he took with him well over $6000 in Confederate notes.[3]

The attitude of Stephen Duncan prior to 1863 was rather typical. By any reasonable definition of Union nationalism there were no more than a handful of Unionist planters in the lower Mississippi Valley before the arrival of the Northern army. The opposition of the gentry to the cause of secession—and it had been considerable along the river—had disappeared with the firing on Fort Sumter. They had become Confederate nationalists. During the following two years local planters invested heavily in Confederate bonds, marched off to battle at the head of regiments they had organized and equipped with their own money, and took prominent positions in the government of the new nation.

Yet, well before the end of the war the Confederate nationalism of the planters in the lower valley had ceased to have any functional meaning. Part of the explanation for this development is fairly well known. It forms a large chapter in the story that goes by the name of declining Confederate morale. Confederate nationalism—or morale—began eroding as the central government in Richmond encroached upon states rights prerogatives. It weakened further as a result of mounting shortages, uncontrollable inflation, and intensifying hardships. Confederate loyalties softened and crumbled even more as news of Union victories began piling up and ultimate defeat loomed increasingly likely. And they gave way almost entirely when the Richmond government began to take on a life of its own (as governments tend to do) and placed its own survival above the concrete interests of the planting class, impressing slaves to work on fortifications and finally calling for an end to slavery itself. To the planters this was a contradiction of Confederate nationalism because it was a betrayal of their welfare and a threat to their dominance.[4]

In the lower Mississippi Valley the cumulative weight of these things became practically unbearable for Southern nationalism after the fall of Vicksburg in July, 1863. What General Kirby Smith said of the civilians west of the Mississippi River held true for the noncombatants immediately to the east of it as well. They were, he complained, "a lukewarm people . . . who appear more intent upon the means of evading the enemy and saving their property than of defending their firesides." He also confessed to some puzzlement as to the nature of their patriotism, which he freely admitted "is beyond my grasp."⁵ But there was nothing mysterious about their national allegiances at all. As the Confederate government proved less able to protect its citizens, they in turn proved less willing to give their government loyalty.

But this was only one side to the story of how the planters in the lower valley fell away from their Confederate allegiances. The other side revolves around the calculated appeals that Federal authorities made to the gentry's self-interest. These appeals doubtless caught the planters by surprise. They seem to have expected harsh treatment at the hands of the conqueror. Most of the gentry abandoned their plantations upon the enemy's approach and sought refuge in the Confederate hinterland, usually in Texas, Alabama, or Georgia. Those who stayed behind offered the Yankees cold disdain and defiance. Only a few were willing to disavow the Confederacy, and even they could not hide that "the presence of such a crowd of 'Yankees' is hateful as poison to them. . . ."⁶ The majority were openly unrepentant. Louisa Quitman Lovell, daughter of the firebrand John A. Quitman and wife of a Confederate captain, was extremely embittered by the occupation. The first time federal officers attended services at her church it was all she could do to restrain her feelings. "I longed to be able to say *something* that would reveal to them how intensely I hated them, . . . my cheeks burned & my heart throbbed—I don't know how I got through the service."⁷

Before much time had elapsed the passions of war had cooled appreciably, however, for federal authorities were unexpectedly conciliatory. The streams of this conciliation rose from several sources: from the natural inclination of Union generals not to disturb the status quo and thereby complicate the movements of their armies; from the desire of federal officials for agreeable society among the local gentry; from the racial prejudices of the invader; and from old-fashioned acquisitiveness—especially from acquisitiveness. Cotton prices were soaring in 1863 to well over $1 a pound, and enterprising individuals of all ranks envisioned wondrous opportunities for financial gain, both legal and otherwise. "Everyone here is crazy with the cotton speculation," observed a young surgeon from Illinois.[8] When added to the desires on the part of local commanders for social stability, racial order, and pleasant company, the profit motive worked powerfully to incline the conqueror away from hard-line policies and toward leniency. Only by resuming cotton growing and reopening the Mississippi trade could these desires be fulfilled and the profits achieved. And only by working closely with the former slaveowners themselves could the plantation economy be resurrected swiftly and efficiently.

Yet all these streams of conciliation seem to have flowed into one major current: the conscious efforts of the Lincoln administration at several levels to undermine the Confederacy and rescusitate Southern Unionism by making calculated appeals to the self-interest of individual Confederates, and this at a time when the government in Richmond was proving increasingly unable to protect the welfare of its citizens. Indeed, some high-ranking Northern officials even believed that the planting class, as well as Confederate authorities, could literally be bribed out of their political allegiances. This was apparently what U.S. Senator Orville Browning had in mind when he maintained that "every Treasurey note we put into the pocket of a rebel makes him, to that extent, interested in the government and its friend, and will become one of the means of destroying the Confederacy."[9] This was likewise what General Lorenzo Thomas meant when he averred, while in the lower Mississippi Valley to take charge of the freedmen, that "the prospect of a sale of two or three hundred bales of cotton, at the present high prices, is a powerful weight in the scale of loyalties."[10] This was also the point General Nathaniel P. Banks was driving at when, as commander of the Department of the Gulf, he argued that "where your treasure is, there will be your heart be also. . . ."[11] And this was the operating premise of Bank's predecessor in Louisiana, General Ben Butler, who, according to one of his lieutenants, tried "to interest every man in business, so that he might come to have a pecuniary regard in the stability and success of the government of the United States."[12]

President Lincoln especially shared this faith in the efficacy of calculated magnanimity. For he seems to have grasped very early in the war the connection between self-interest and political loyalties, and to have realized that Union nationalism was a dynamic force that could be strengthened or attenuated under the proper stimuli. His peace and reconstruction policy reflected this understanding. The policy itself was complex and ambidexterous. Essentially it sought to detach Southern allegiances from the Confederate government and reattach them to the Federal government, while at the same time redefining the Union as he moved to abolish slavery. Positive appeals to self-interest were a critical part of his program. They consisted of offers of privileges and immunities, ranging from protection of property to permits to travel, and authorizations to trade and lease, in exchange for a pledge by the planters of future loyalty to the Federal government. Implicit in these latter appeals, and often made explicit by many commanders on the scene, was the promise that Washington would uphold the traditional authority of the planting class. Later in the war, in December, 1863, when he unveiled his ten percent plan of reconstruction, whereby state governments could be formed in the seceded areas whenever ten percent of the white adults had taken the oath of amnesty, Lincoln tried to fashion an instrument for holding some Southerners to their renewed Federal allegiances while luring yet others away from their Confederate loyalties. According to one recent student of Lincoln's thought, nearly every aspect of the president's peace and reconstruction policy was based on the assumption that "the South would be seduced into peace via the economic charms of the Union. . . ."[13]

Many of the details of this peace strategy were worked out by commanders in the field, whom Lincoln customarily entrusted with as much discretion as they could handle. The principal inducement held out to planters in the occupied areas was the opportunity to participate in official programs to restore the cotton economy. In the Department of the Gulf, for instance, General Nathaniel P. Banks invited sugar planters to aid federal officials in drawing up guidelines for the new "free labor" system. He hoped, by showing respect for the experience of the elite and implementing many of their suggestions, to tie their interests to the fate of the Union. General Lorenzo Thomas, in charge farther upriver, modeled his regulations after those of General Banks, assuring planters that the slave labor system embodied the wisdom of the past and therefore should be closely followed. Under the program he introduced, hours of work, gangs, drivers, and overseers all remained much the same as before the war. Runaway laborers were returned to their former masters and compelled to be obedient.[14] James McKaye, one of the members of the Freedmen's Inquiry Commission, reported that on many of the estates in the lower Mississippi Valley even whipping was condoned.[15] The entire program aimed to ensure the planters that upon restoration of the Union depended the restoration of their material fortunes.

The leasing program federal authorities devised for the maintenance of abandoned and confiscated plantations along the Mississippi River worked in an analogous fashion. Its purpose was avowedly political: to line the banks of the river with a loyal population. Many of these "loyalists" were expected to come from the North. The wish to transform the South by overwhelming her natives with Yankee settlers, much as England had once tried to do in Ireland, was very strong at this time. Yet just as potent was the desire of Union officials to recruit the conquered

planters into the ranks of loyalism. In order to operate a plantation or lease it out to others, one had first to sign an oath of
allegiance to the Federal government, or at least take on a "loyal"
partner. Otherwise the occupying authorities would rent the estate directly to the fortune seekers then crowding into the area to
take advantage of the high price of cotton.[16] Although this was
the iron-fist-in-the-glove approach, the glove was pure velvet.
Substantial sums of guaranteed income could be realized by plantation owners through the leasing program, and not a few of the
gentry seem to have grasped this fact quite readily. Over one-
fourth of the plantations rented under the supervision of the
Treasury Department in the lower Mississippi Valley were
leased directly from their owners. The rents were usually hand-
some. Alfred Vidal Davis, for example, received $5,000 in both
1864 and 1865 for the lease of one of his plantations in Concordia
parish, Louisiana. Stephen Duncan, who, it will be recalled, had
declared in 1861 that it was every Southerner's duty "to unite in
the vigorous prosecution of the war," by 1864 was trying to rent
one of his places to the enemy for $15,000 annually. As he in-
formed one Union general, a *"reliable* man, who would take *a
valuable* plantation, with *everything* on it, labor included, . . .
can be accommodated, on application to Yours very truly."[17]

Even after the cotton had been picked, local planters received
valued assistance in processing and selling the staple. Authorities
gave them preferred access to the available gins, leaving the
"poorer classes" with little choice but to sell their own small
output to wealthier neighbors, and they readily issued them permits for shipping their cotton to market.[18]

The Federal policy of calculated magnanimity employed the
personal touch as well. The authorities took pains to see that
planters and their families were treated with deference and con-
sideration. Guards were placed over the homes of the Natchez
gentry so as to protect them from theft and vandalism by the
soldiers of either army.[19] One union general sent two Northern
enlisted men to prison for 20 years because they stole $1,000 in

silver from the estate of John C. Jenkins.[20] "To give the devil his due," confessed Kate Aubrey of Adams County, Mississippi, in February, 1864, "I must say that some of the Federal troops have behaved very gentlemanly towards us,"[21] She may have been referring to the concerts that were regularly staged for the entertainment of the local citizenry.[22] General Thomas often placed his official boat, piloted by one of his sons, at the personal disposal of the large planters along the river. He had made their acquaintance before the war, and when he returned he announced his readiness to do everything within his power "to help out his old friends,"[23]

Coming at a time when the powers of the Richmond government were on the wane, this Federal solicitude had a powerful effect on the attitude and conduct of the old elite. Even the defiantly unrepentant were won over. Six months after her blood had boiled and cheeks had burned at the sight of Union officers in attendance at her church, Mrs. Louisa Quitman Lovell felt her temperature drop considerably, The cooling began when a federal official with "much influence among the authorities at Vicksburg" persuaded her to take the oath of amnesty so that he might help her sell her cotton and lease the family plantation. After the cotton had been sold for $30,000 her mood toward the conqueror had grown warm again, but this time on the scale of cordiality. Regarding the Union general, Henry Slocumb, who had helped her with the transaction, she wrote: "how fortunate we are in having such a good friend. You cannot imagine how good, how kind he is to us all. He is truly a high minded, noble man! He comes out every evening as he says to take care of us at night—I don't know what we should have done without his kind assistance." Probably not have rented the plantation for $12,000, which was done in November, 1864. By the eve of Appomattox Mrs. Lovell was marvelling at the liberality of the very Yankees she had once hated with an intensity she could scarcely conceal. "A wonderful change has come over everything," she wrote "I have got *protection* for the woods etc & *every body* is *very kind* & polite."[24]

This was how the federal peace policy of calculated magnanimity was administered within occupied territory. Beyond Federal lines, however, within the Confederate hinterland as well as in that no-man's land between the two armies, a more indirect method of appealing to planter self-interest was employed. The method consisted of various inducements and facilities to engage in the illicit wartime trade in cotton. The Union military was generally not enthusiastic about this policy, nor were the War and Treasury Departments very approving, and Congress was almost always dubious about its wisdom. The contraband trade usually ended up feeding and clothing the very armies the Union was trying to starve into submission. It was an open secret, for example, that occupied Memphis was "a greater outfitting point for Confederate armies than Nassau."[25] But influential political and commercial interest were eager to see the commerce carried on—some spokesmen for the New England textile industry wanted free trade with the Confederacy—and President Lincoln himself privately believed, as he confided to Secretary of the Navy Gideon Welles, that the interbelligerent trade in cotton would be a means by which "important persons in the Confederacy were to be converted."[26] Despite the blockade, then, as early as the fall of 1861 the President began issuing special trade permits to speculators who desired to bring cotton from beyond Federal lines. By the last year of the war, in September, 1864, he had even moved to put the commerce upon a fairly open basis, promulgating executive orders that allowed owners of cotton from within the Confederacy to receive three-fourths of the market value for their crop and to carry back within enemy lines goods and supplies, supposedly nonmilitary, valued at one-third of the purchase price of that same cotton. The only stipulation was that the traders sign oaths of future loyalty to the Union.[27]

The result was a brisk interbelligerent trade that carried

Southern cotton north in return for badly needed clothes, food, and medicines. Between 1864 and 1865 the number of bales of cotton reaching New Orleans had increased sixfold, and at one period so much contraband cotton was passing through Baton Rouge on its way to the Crescent City that two large steamers were required to transport it daily. Not surprisingly, Confederate patriotism as well as cotton flowed outward on the stream of commerce. The privations planters had experienced, the hardships they had endured, the near desperate condition of their families and farms, understandably caused many planters in the hinterlands to warmly greet the speculators who came among them offering high prices for their cotton not to mention a variety of goods that had become practically unobtainable. John Winters tells of hundreds of Louisianians of greater or lesser prominence who did not hesitate to take the oath in order to engage in the trade. This was in the Florida Parishes, but Confederate civilians elsewhere in the lower valley were just as willing to sign the same pledge so as to secure the same privilege. The oaths allowed them to get the permits that were required to ship in cotton from beyond federal lines.[28]

Confederate officials were not unmindful of the demoralizing effects of the trade. Yet, they were largely powerless to bring it under control. Part of their problem involved the partisan rangers they dispatched to curb the traffic and tame the lessees: the guerillas quickly took to exacting tribute from the cotton shippers, seizing the property and goods of innocent noncombatants, and collecting "rent" from the Northern planters who were happy enough to buy protection considering the circumstances.[29] But the main difficulty in the way of suppressing the trade was the Confederacy's own dependence upon it for essential supplies. As early as 1862 the Confederate Commissary and War Departments began conniving in the commerce in order to feed and clothe the armies in the field, and by the last year of the war they too, like Lincoln, tried to place the commerce on a regular basis.[30] Thus, a Baton Rouge merchant had permission, authorized independently by federal and Confederate officials on the *same* document, to operate on both sides of the lines,[31] Thus, too, U.S. Navy gunboats carried cotton speculators directly into Confederate General Richard Taylor's lines on the Red River, where the traders and their Union army escorts were feted by Confederate officers overseeing the transaction. The most famous example of the two armies bartering with and killing one another simultaneously was in the east, when Grant was trying to strangle the life out of Lee's army in the Petersburg entrenchments. For a brief period during the siege Northern cotton speculators were supplying the hard-pressed Confederate army with boots and bacon, until Grant caught wind of the trade and brought it to a halt.[32] Such episodes lend plausibility to an observation made in Memphis in 1863: "The war is carried on apparently for no purpose now by those actually engaged in it, but to create opportunities for plunder and fraud."[33]

This is certainly one way to look at the trade. The profits available from trafficking in wartime cotton, as Ludwell Johnson has demonstrated, gave rise to a degree of official corruption on both sides that was truly shocking. One United States Senator who investigated the commerce shuddered to make the findings public. Another facetiously told official Washington to withdraw all your Army, and enlist a large force of Yankee peddlers . . . to go down there and trade them all out; clean them out in trade." The malfeasance was widespread.[34] But to look at the cotton trade in this light only is to miss its true significance. Lincoln realized corruption would be a likely byproduct of his peace policy, but he believed it was a price worth paying. ". . . if pecuniary greed can be made to aid us in such an effort," he is quoted as having once remarked in this connection, "let us be thankful that so much good can be got out of pecuniary greed."[35] There may have been something to his faith. For the inability of the Confederate government to survive without this trade, let alone bring it under control, starkly announced Richmond's powerlessness any longer to protect or advance the welfare of its people, especially the planter class. That power had effectively passed to the federal government, which was making skillful use of it to hasten the disintegration of Confederate national loyalties.

This is not to say that the Lincoln administration ever achieved its stated objective of reconstituting patriotic feelings for the Union among the gentry. Even though they were falling away from their Confederate loyalties, few planters were prepared to transfer their allegiances unequivocally to the Union. They hesitated in part for fear of alienating unrepentant friends and relatives. They also paused because the signals from Washington were ambiguous. There were those clear reassurances of federal intentions to preserve the plantation and confirm traditional patterns of authority, but just as unmistakeable were the mounting signs that the new Union would be without slavery.

But mainly the planters equivocated about their allegiances because the federal government was never fully able during the war to protect their welfare. Confederate guerillas still roamed freely in the twilight zone between the two armies, and they had to be reckoned with. "We could stand the Yankees pretty well," observed a Louisiana woman in late 1864, "but to have Negroes, Grey backs & Jay hawkers besides, puts a body to their wits end to keep body and soul together."[36] "Our principal diff'y," wrote one planter from Adams county, Mississippi, in November, 1863, "is the position we occupy outside the picket lines, which prevents us from getting the necessary supplies & yet close enough to be in hearing & in sight of the Federals & what is worse in danger of inroads from the Confederates."[37] Travelling down the Louisiana side of the river after the war, Whitelaw Reid noted many cotton gins which had been destroyed by guerillas determined that "the Yankees or men that should stay at home and be friendly with the Yankees, shouldn't make money out of them."[38]

In fact, the Union government could not even keep its own soldiers in harness. Bored, vindictive, and with little to gain from the good graces of the gentry, they were constantly on the lookout for opportunities to loot and pillage. Joshua James of "Ion," a plantation of 1300 acres in Tensas Parish, Louisiana, was guaranteed protection of his property by Union officials in early April, 1863. But a few days later soldiers overran his land, destroying his cotton gin, steam engine, and family carriage, and confiscating all his grain and livestock.[39] The estate of a neighbor, Haller Nutt, an avowed Unionist, was left in ruins, "supposed to have been done principally by the stragglers of the Army."[40] Stern penalties for thievery were introduced, bu plunder continued anyway, some soldiers insisting "they stole only those chickens and pigs that refused the Northern loyalty test."[41]

So the gentry remained coy about their public allegiances. Toward the federal loyalty oaths their attitude was rather casual. Some planters swore loyalty "to save their property," then rode off to participate in raids against Yankee lessees.[42] Others avoided the oath but used their wealth and charm to secure its benefits. One Union general reported frequent invitations to "very brilliant, splendid dinners, suppers, all that sort of thing with speeches, songs, mirth and hilarity."[43] Or they sold their cotton to or through acquaintances who had pledged their loyalty. In one week in November, 1863, William Newton Mercer realized more than $90,000 on the sale of cotton to his close friend, Levin R. Marshall.[44] A novel approach was taken by some planters in Wilkinson county, Mississippi. For $1 they "sold" their cotton to an Englishmen, Charles Lewis, who promised to carry it to Liverpool for them for half the profits. Theoretically his status as a neutral would allow Lewis to apply to either government for damages should the cotton be destroyed in transit.[45]

The uncertainties in the situation clearly discouraged firm commitments. When approached by General Lorenzo Thomas to take the lead in forming a loyalist government in Mississippi during the war, the old line Whig William Sharkey politely demurred. Judge Sharkey felt "the undercurrent of Unionism [needed] to show itself more decisively before any action should be had," by which he undoubtedly meant that the federal government had to establish its control more completely before he would get off the fence.[46]

But if Washington had not yet acquired the power to reunionize the occupied areas of the wartime South, it was nonetheless able to destabilize the Richmond government by means not exclusively military. Beyond all question the policy of calculated magnanimity did hasten the disintegration of Confederate nationalism. The demoralization can be measured only in subtle ways: by the growing readiness of men to desert from the army or evade conscription in order to engage in cotton trading; by the increasing determination of planters to grow cotton instead of the provision crops that Confederate officials urged be raised; by the widening circulation of federal greenbacks within Southern lines because speculators refused to accept their Confederate counterparts; and by a thousand and one other minor ways in which Southern planters lost vital sympathy in the cause of the government they had but a short time before called into being.[47] James Lusk Alcorn made much of his refusal to take the oath, saying he had already given his word and was too much of a gentleman to go back on it now. But formal allegiances are one thing, functional loyalties another. While observing a strict allegiance to the Confederacy, Alcorn not only smuggled cotton to the enemy, but hobnobbed with Union generals in Helena, Arkansas, and helped federal gunboats find navigable routes through the streams and bayous in his home county. Are we to take him at his word or judge him by his behavior?[48] And what are we to make of D. B. Nailer, who described himself as "the most uncompromising Rebel in [Warren] county" but who nonetheless petitioned Jefferson Davis in early 1864 for the release of three captured Union soldiers? "These men were given to me by [Union] Gen. McPherson as guards," he explained, "and but for them my family would have been insulted daily by the Fed. soldiers & thieves attached to the army."[49] Where did Nailer's real loyalties lie in this instance? Certainly not with Richmond.

But whither the nationalistic feeling of the gentry if it had become unmoored from the Confederacy but had not yet found anchor in the Union? The evidence is suggestive that it sought safe harbor in those concrete attachments to family, property, class, and community which nationalism subsumes but does not obliterate because they remain primary. Lillian Pereyra has put it rather well in explaining the apparently unpatriotic conduct of James Alcorn. Caught in the cross-currents of war, Alcorn and "many others in similar circumstances simply retreated to the firm ground of immediate, tangible loyalties which they could serve close to home, and which served them."[50] This may have been selfish behavior, but it is not surprising behavior. Nor is it necessarily deplorable. Potter was correct to remind us that nationalism does not transcend self-interest but springs from it. He was probably even justified in believing that Confederate nationalism grew more from common interest than common culture. The cultural ingredients of Southern nationalism appear to have been weak to begin with. Otherwise it is hard to understand how appeals to self-interest could have broken it down as easily as they did.

One Mississippian who lived through the war described it as a time that was "too utilitarian for such Quixotic patriotism as some preached and but few practiced."[51] What he was really saying is that proponents of nationalism can disregard the calculus of self-interest only at their peril. Those planters in the lower valley who, to paraphrase James L. Roark, chose the homestead over the homeland,[52] illustrate this truth with unmistakeable clarity.

Many Thousands Gone: Black Southerners and the Confederacy

LEON F. LITWACK

Some seventy-five years after the Civil War, two white women approached a small house on Camp Street in New Orleans. They had been told that it was the home of Mary Harris, an elderly black woman who had once been a slave on a sugar plantation in Louisiana and who might be willing to talk about those days for the WPA oral history project. "Sure I remember slavery times," she told them. "I was a big girl, turned eleven. I used to pull the fan that kep' off the flies while the white folks was eatin'. It wasn't hard work but my arms used to get tired—'specially at dinner when they set so long at the table." She had never been whipped, she said, because she had performed her tasks and had never talked back. "My ma tol' me she was brutally beaten an' she was bitter all her life."

When the two women returned the next day to continue the interview, they found Mary Harris's son barring their way. "Slavery!" he exclaimed. "Why are you concerned about such stuff? It's bad enough for it to have existed and when we can't forget it there is no need of rehashing it." The women explained that they only wished to preserve the reminiscences of old people about the Old South and the War. Making clear his own bitterness about that past, the son reminded them of the stories of brutality he had heard from his mother. The two visitors replied that all slaveholders had not behaved in such ways. Even if slavery had been "unfortunate," as they had told his mother the previous day, "old slaves still tell of their love for 'ole Miss' and 'ole Marse,' and the loyalty and love existing between them could never have been created in raucuos hearts."

The son remained unmoved. "Yes'm, I'm bitter and the more I think about it the madder I get. Look at me. They say I could pass for white. My mother is bright too. And why? Because the man who owned and sold my mother was her father. But that's not all. That man I hate with every fibre of my body and why? A brute like that who could sell his own child into unprincipled hands is a beast—the power, just because he had the power, and the thirst for money."

Having made his point, the son finally agreed to permit the two women to see his mother again. But they had heard enough. "After such a tirade we were afraid, deciding that 'discretion was the better part of valor.' It was our first experience with a mad-man."

For generations, our perceptions of slavery, the Confederate South, and the Civil War were dominated by the recollections of white men and women. If the black Southerner revealed his thoughts about such subjects, he did so invariably through white intermediaries. And, like the two women in New Orleans, such intermediaries tended to value blacks primarily for their pictur-esque qualities, viewing them as appendages of Southern soci-ety, as lovable Uncles and Aunties whose behavior was as easily explicable as it was quaint. To think of slaves who had betrayed their masters was to think of slaves who had not been them-selves, who had been misled, who had lost their minds. That assumption was commonplace during the Civil War. After a Richmond slave denounced Jefferson Davis and refused to work for any white man, a local editor demanded that he "be whipped every day until he confesses what white man put these notions in his head." For whites to believe anything else was to compromise their self-esteem and call into question the prevailing conviction that slavery was the best possible condition for black people. To

pretend that the Yankees provoked slave transgressions proved
to be a highly popular explanation of wartime behavior. "The
poor negroes don't do us any harm except when they are put
up to it," one Southern woman observed. "Even when they murdered that white man and quartered him, I believe pernicious
teachings were responsible." Whether during the war or in its
aftermath, Southern whites refused to believe that the Negroes
they knew so well might have developed their own norms of
behavior and evolved their own concepts of freedom, their own
sense of individual autonomy and self-worth.

In the literature of the War for Southern Independence, the
"unfaithful" Negro was accorded only passing notice, if any at all.
The slaves who would be commemorated in song, verse, and
bronze were those who had fulfilled white expectations, who had
stood steadfastly by their masters and mistresses, who had shared
with them the wartime privations and tragedies, and who had
extended no welcome to the Yankee invaders. "Could any people
have expected more of a so-called servile race?" asked one grateful white woman. "Is it strange that we should wish to erect
monuments to the Slaves of the South and to the memory of the
dear "Old Black Mammy'?" The citizens of Fort Mill, South
Carolina, did precisely that. In a park dedicated to the Confederate war dead, they placed an unusual statue, with the names of
ten slaves engraved on it; the stone carvings on each side de-
picted a black man, seated at the edge of a field of grain, grasping
a scythe in his hand, and an elderly black woman, seated on the
steps of a plantation house, holding in her arms a white child.
The inscription proclaimed the war as it would be relived in the
mind of the white South.

Dedicated to
The Faithful Slaves
Who, Loyal to a Sacred Trust,
Toiled for the Support
Of the Army, with Matchless
Devotion, and with Sterling
Fidelity Guarded Our Defenseless

Homes, Women and Children, During
The Struggle for the Principles
Of Our Confederate States of America

While white Southerners revered such memories, black Southerners harbored some different thoughts. When informed that
the town in which he resided had passed a resolution praising the
wartime loyalty of slaves like himself, an elderly freedman
thought it a rather amusing gesture. "They needn't have done
that," he remarked, "for every now and then we were falling
behind a stump or into a corner of the fence and praying for the
Union soldiers." They did that much and more.

To my knowledge, there are no monuments in the South to the
more than 100,000 black Southerners who fought in the war—
that is, to those who took up arms against the Confederacy and
helped to bring the new Southern nation to its knees. Near Port
Hudson, off the road between Baton Rouge and Natchez, I did
once visit a United States National Cemetery where 3,804 Union
soldiers are buried, 3,262 of them in graves marked "unknown."
The WPA state guide neglected to mention the race of the buried
soldiers, but the inscription on the gravestones made that clear
enough; almost all of them had fought with the United States
Colored Troops. If the white South chose to ignore these men,
most of them native sons, neither was it likely to erect any monuments to the tens of thousands of black Southerners—men and
women—who found individual ways to undermine the Confederate war effort, whether as spies, informants, and guides, or by
the withdrawal of their labor.

Neither in Southern nor in Northern accounts of the Civil War
did blacks play much more than a passive role. In 1961, for
example, the first year of the Civil War Centennial, the Mississippi Department of Archives and History published an impres-
sive volume, *Mississippi in the Confederacy: As They Saw It*, the
story of the war "told by those who lived through it." But to read
the volume is to know only of how white Mississippians viewed

the war. In the more than 1000 pages that make up Henry Steele
Commager's *The Blue and the Gray: The Story of the Civil War
as Told by Participants*, the black voice is as effectively stilled.
The Freedmen's Memorial Monument in Washington, D.C.,
projects the vision of emancipation that would be inculcated into
the minds of generations of Americans. The martyred President
is standing, grasping in one hand the Emancipation Proclamation
while the other hand is poised above the head of a humble,
kneeling slave, the shackles on his wrists broken. Only in retro-
spect did Frederick Douglass come to object to the monument
he had helped to dedicate in 1876. What troubled him was the
impression it conveyed that the slaves had waited passively for
the white man to break the chains of bondage. Douglass knew
better, as did those slaves who had seized the initiative to liber-
ate themselves, as did those white families who had seen their
property transformed into unrecognizable men and women.

Without slavery, there would have been no Confederate States
of America. The enslavement of black men and women went to
the heart of its existence, sustained it in its desperate struggle for
survival, defined it as a nation. No less a personage than its vice-
president, Alexander H. Stephens, pronounced slavery the "cornerstone" of the Confederate South. The Union, he noted,
"rested upon the assumption of the equality of the races." The
Confederate States of America, on the other hand, "is founded
upon exactly the opposite idea; its foundations are laid, its cornerstone rests, upon the great truth that the negro is not equal to
the white man; that slavery, subordination to the superior race, is
his natural and normal condition." The white South echoed
Stephens's words. In the patriotic oratory that ushered in the
war, slavery was pronounced "a tower of strength" that would
assure the ultimate triumph of independence. It was slavery that
welded the Southern states together, and it was slave labor that
would enable the new nation to succeed and to prosper. "In the
present crisis," a Montgomery, Alabama, newspaper boasted,

"our enemies will be likely to find that the 'moral cancer,' about which their orators are so fond of prating, is really one of the most effective weapons employed against them by the South."

The assumption that the Confederacy and slave labor shared a common destiny was proven correct. Both expired in the crucible of a bloody and destructive war. Few if any experiences in American lives have been felt so deeply, so intensely by so many, and few are as replete with paradox, ambiguity, and irony, with both tragedy and triumph. From the very outset of the war, black Southerners were placed in an anomolous and dangerous position—in an impossible position. On the one hand, they were the cause of the war; on the other, they were necessary for the war's success—that is, their labor and loyalty were essential to the Confederacy. But could they be trusted? The answer came slowly in some cases, quickly in others: the more desperate the Confederate cause became, the more the white South depended on the labor and loyalty of its blacks. And the more they were needed, the less they could be trusted.

Neither whites nor blacks were untouched by the physical and emotional demands of the war. Both races suffered, and each evinced some sympathy for the plight of the other. But there was a critical difference, and that difference grew in importance with each passing month. If slaves evinced a compassion for beleaguered masters and mistresses, if they deplored the ravagement of the land and crops by Union soldiers who brutalized and looted whites and blacks alike, many of these same slaves and still others came to appreciate at some moment in the war that in the very suffering and defeat of their "white folks" lay their only hope for freedom. That revelation was no less far-reaching in its implications than the acknowledgment by white Southerners that they were facing danger on both sides—from the Yankees and from their own blacks. "We have already been twice betrayed by negroes," Joseph LeConte lamented, as he made his way to the safety of Confederate lines; "we avoid them as carefully as we do Yankees." No less distraught, the mistress of a plantation in the Abbeville district of South Carolina wondered how the remaining whites could possibly survive if the home guard was called up to combat the Yankees. "If the men are going, then awful things are coming, and I don't want to stay. My God, the women and children, it will be murder and ruin. There are many among the black people and they only want a chance."

The tensions and tragedies introduced into the lives of white families during the Civil War made them seem, in the eyes of their slaves, less than omnipotent. Rarely, after all, had slaves perceived their owners so beleaguered, so helpless, so utterly at the mercy of circumstances over which they had no control. It was the kind of vulnerability a slave could readily understand. If privation, betrayed expectations, fear of the unknown, and the forced separation from loved ones were new experiences for many whites, they were not for many slaves. To witness the anguish of white men and women experiencing some of the same personal tragedies and disruptions they had visited upon others no doubt generated considerable ambivalence in the slave quarters, if not some private or shared gratification. Levi Ashley, a former Mississippi slave, sorted out his thoughts some years later about the plight of his "white folks" during and after the war. He had worked for "de hardes' man ever lived" and for a mistress who had been equally "mean an' hard." The war left its mark on the plantation in ways he could easily appreciate.

> When Marse John was in de war he had his arm shot off an' afte' he come back, he didn' live long. Miss Elviry an' her mother, Miss Fanny, was lef' alone. Dey sho' got to be po' folks. Dey had to sell dey beddin' an' furniture in de house fer suppo't. All de old slaves sho' was glad to hear it. Dey was so mean to 'em. You know, lady, 'whut goes over de Devil's backbone is boun' to pass under his stomach'—an' dey got whut was comin' to 'em.

Contrary to the legends of "docility" and "rebelliousness," the variety of slave personalities does not permit any easy division of the nearly four million enslaved blacks into Uncle Toms and Nat

Turners. Rebelliousness, resistance, accommodation, and submission might manifest themselves at different times in the same
slave, depending on his or her own perception of reality. Few
slaves, no matter how effusively they professed their fidelity to
"marse" and "missus," did not contain within them a capacity for
outrage. Whether or not that outrage ever surfaced was the
terrible reality every white man and woman had to live with and
could never really escape. The experiences of war and emancipation made this abundantly clear, playing upon and exacerbating
white fears and fantasies that were as old as slavery itself. The
tension could prove to be unbearable. Midway through the war,
a Southern white woman noted in her diary that a room in the
house had accidentally caught fire. "But we at once thought Jane
[the cook] was wreaking vengeance on us all by trying to burn us
out. We would not have been surprised to have her slip up &
stick any of us in the back."

The importance of the nearly four million slaves could not be
measured in economic terms alone. What black novelist Ralph
Ellison said of the black presence in the South one century later
was no less true of the war years: "Southern whites cannot walk,
talk, sing, conceive of laws or justice, think of sex, love, the
family, or freedom without responding to the presence of
Negroes." Whether by their conversations or daily conduct,
slaveholding families revealed a relationship with their blacks
that was riddled with ambiguity, doubt, and suspicion. No matter how much they flaunted their pretensions to security and
professed to believe in the fidelity of their own blacks, the doubts
and the apprehension surfaced with every rumor of an uprising,
with ever case of insubordination and desertion, with every perceived change in the demeanor of their slaves.

The almost studied indifference of some slaves was perhaps
most troubling of all. For white families to determine how their
slaves felt about the war could be a downright frustrating and
exasperating experience. To listen to their slaves' professions of
fidelity was seldom as reassuring as it should have been. If white

families complained with increasing frequency of the deceit-
fulness of their slaves, that suggested how well the blacks played
their roles, invoking the "darky act" at the appropriate moment.
If some slaves internalized the ritual of deference, few whites
knew for certain. The slave's "mask of meekness," Ralph Ellison
has suggested, "conceals the wisdom of one who has learned the
secret of saying the 'yes' which accomplishes the expressive
'no.'" Generations of blacks made the same point when they
taught their children, "Be sho' you knows 'bout all you tells, but
don't tell all you knows," or when they sang,

Got one mind for white folks to see,
'Nother for what I know is me;
He don't know, he don't know my mind.

Louis Manigault, the Georgia planter, conceded as much when
he reflected on his wartime experience, "So deceitful is the
Negro that as far as my own experience extends I could never in a
single instance decipher his character."

To endure enslavement, black men and women had learned
how to placate the fears of the white owners, how to stroke their
egos, how to anticipate their moves and moods. During the Civil
War, when the white family's temperament fluctuated even
more violently, it became imperative for the slave to remain
circumspect in his views, to feign stupidity or indifference at the
right moment, to mask his feelings, to adopt the appropriate
facial expressions and gestures in his responses to whites, to
exploit the various ploys that made up the "darky act"—the hat in
hand, the down-cast eyes, the shuffling feet, the fumbling words.
When questioned about the war, slaves shaped their responses to
the tone of the question and the requirements of the occasion,
and some sought refuge in a pretense of incomprehension.
"Why, you see, master," one elderly slave responded, "'taint for
an old nigger like me to know anything 'bout politics." But when
he was pressed further to indicate his preference for the Union or
the Confederacy, he smiled and carefully phrased his reply, "I'm

on de Lord's side." If the "darky act" was performed for Yankees and Confederates alike, that reflected a slave's sense of reality. The Civil War would not last forever, a Texas slave advised his son, but "our forever was going to be spent living among the Southerners, after they got licked."

No matter how cautiously a master screened news of the war and emancipation, slaves employed time-tested devices to obtain and communicate information. "Shucks," a former Louisiana slave recalled, "we knew ev'rything de master talked er bout. The house girl would tell us an we would pass it er round. Dats how we knew dat master was er fraid of de yankees." Even if the "grapevine telegraph" broke down, slaves possessed an extraordinary insight into the minds and moods of their "white folks." To gaze at their faces, to feel the growing tension was to know how the war was progressing, that the expected early victory had become instead a prolonged, costly, and apparently fated slaughter. Even if the precise causes of the war remained unclear, what was at stake became increasingly clear. Slaves remained reticent about openly revealing their feelings. But they found it increasingly difficult to mask them, particularly as the outcome of the war became more predictable. The more perceptive masters and mistresses sensed the changes. On some plantations, the prayer meetings in the quarters and fields were noticeably louder and more effusive; songs about the war and freedom suddenly surfaced as well, some of them composed for the occasion, many of them variations on older songs whose contents had seemed innocuous to whites.

Even if the words of many slave spirituals and songs did not change during the Civil War, their immediacy did, and that was often reflected in the emphasis with which certain phrases were intoned. Near the end of the war, with Lee's surrender imminent, a white woman in the Alabama black belt overheard a service conducted by slaves. With particular fervor, they were singing:

Where oh where is the good old Daniel,
Where oh where is the good old Daniel,
Who was cast in the lions den?
Safe now in the promised land;
By and by we'll go home to meet him,
By and by we'll go home to meet him,
Way over in the promised land.

Listening to the voices, she "could almost imagine they were on
wing for 'the promised land' as they seemed to throw all the
passion of their souls into the refrain." Whatever meaning she
chose to attach to the words in the song, the entire scene only
reinforced her feelings of despondency and impending disaster.
"I . . . seemed to see the mantle of our lost cause descending." It
was as though these slaves, in their own devious way, understood
even better than she did or could admit to herself that "the
promised land" lay in the ruins of the Confederacy. And in
"Many Thousands Gone," a spiritual composed during the war,
slaves would begin to define that "promised land" as a release
from the most oppressive aspects of bondage: "No more peck
o'corn for me," "No more driver's lash for me," "No more pint
o'salt for me," "No more hundred lash for me," and "No more
mistress' call for me."

To reach that "promised land," flight to the North had become
unnecessary. The proximity of Union soldiers, not the Emancipation Proclamation, made the critical difference in most instances.
Every plantation, every farm, every community had its version of
how the slaves responded. For some masters and mistresses, the
behavior of individual slaves was inexplicable, for others a
confirmation of what they had long suspected. What made the
"faithful few" so exemplary, in the eyes of the white South, were
the slaves who fled to the Union lines without the slightest warning, the servants who turned over the house and barn keys to the
Yankees, the slaves who piloted the troops to where the family
valuables had been secreted (often the same slaves who had

helped to hide them), the slaves who told the Yankees everything, and the slaves who vented their bitterness on the most
glaring and accessible symbols of their enslavement—the Big
House and the cotton gin. John F. Andrews, an Alabama planter,
stood by helplessly while his slaves assisted the Union soldiers in
burning his residence and gin house. "The 'faithful slave' is about
played out," he observed afterwards. "They are the most
treacherous, brutal, and ungrateful race on the globe."

More than any government proclamation, the slaves themselves undermined the authority of the planter class. How they
chose to do so—and when—varied with each slave. How
slaveholding whites chose to make sense out of what was happen-
ing around them assumed a more familiar and uniform pattern.
The terms used by masters and mistresses to describe the disaffection of enslaved black workers—"insolence," "impertinence,"
"impudence," "ingratitude," "betrayal," "desertion," "demoralization"—suggest how many of them perceived the "moment of
truth." In the past, such terms had been employed to denote
slave transgressions or departures from expected behavior. During the war, however, they took on added dimensions, as they
recorded the very destruction of the slave order. To talk about
"ingratitude" was to describe slaves who "defected" without a
word to their masters. To talk about "insolence," "impudence,"
and "impertinence" was to describe slaves who refused to obey
orders and to submit to punishment. (To a Virginia white woman,
the blacks were acting "very independent and impudent," and
like most whites she equated the two traits.) To talk about "de-
moralized" slaves was to describe slaves who were unwilling to
work "as usual." To talk about a "rebellion" or a "state of mutiny"
was to describe slaves who staged plantation strikes or slowdowns
and who in some instances seized control of the plantations,
ousting the overseers left in charge. To talk about "betrayal" was
invariably to report the behavior of slaves in whom masters and
mistresses had reposed the greatest trust and confidence. The
plaintive cries of "betrayal" and "desertion" were heard most

often, perhaps because they were the least comprehensible:
"Those we loved best and who loved us best—as we thought—
were the first to leave us." Neither "rebellious" nor "faithful" in
the fullest sense of those terms, most slaves seemed to have
balanced the habit of obedience against the intense desire for
freedom. But as the war progressed, few owners found themselves able to predict with any confidence when the habit of
obedience would become less compelling than the desire for
freedom.

What the Civil War did was to sweep away the pretenses,
dissolve the illusions, lay bare the tensions and instability inher-
ent in the master-slave relationship, and reveal the many-sided
personalities of enslaved black men and women. It taught the
masters who claimed to "know" the Negro best that they knew
him least of all, that they had mistaken the slave's outward demeanor for his inner feelings, his docility for contentment, his
deference and accommodation for submission. Few sensed this
more clearly than Louis Manigault, when he came to assess the
wartime conduct of his slaves. The slave he had esteemed most
highly, who had been his "constant companion" for thirty years,
had been the first to create trouble. Subsequent "instances of
ingratitude" persuaded Manigault that he could place no
confidence in any of his slaves. "In too numerous instances those
we esteemed the most have been the first to desert us." And
when Manigault returned to the plantation after the war, he
found his newly freed slaves even less recognizable. "I almost
imagined myself with Chinese, Malays or even the Indians in the
interior of the Philippine Islands."

For whites and blacks alike, the Civil War was an experience
as traumatic and far-reaching as any in their lives. The Confederate States of America would assume legendary proportions in the
annals and minds of white Southerners. But for black men and
women, the ultimate significance of the Confederacy lay in its
destruction. What for generations of whites remained a heroic
struggle for independence took on a very different meaning for

black southerners. To have prolonged the life of the Confederacy was to have prolonged their own enslavement and debasement. Understandibly, few of them could embrace such a cause with any degree of enthusiasm, even if it was rooted in a southland they called their home. When he first heard of the act to recruit blacks for the Confederate Army, a Virginia slave could no longer restrain his emotions. "I never felt at liberty to speak my mind until they passed an act to put colored men into the army. That wrought upon my feelings so I couldn't but cry. . . . They asked me if I would fight for my country. I said, 'I have no country.'"

Long after Appomattox, the Civil War would be relived in the American imagination. Historians, novelists, playwrights, and screenwriters would evoke a variety of images, with the proud and devastated Confederacy providing the kind of material of which great tragedies and romances are woven. Perhaps the most pervasive embellishment of the southern mystique was *Gone With the Wind,* a literary and cinematic glorification of the Confederacy. In reviewing this historic epic, Henry Steele Commager, a distinguished historian, suggested that this nation had truly lost something in the demise of the Old South. What was gone with the wind, Commager lamented, was "a way of life and of living, something deeply rooted, genuine and good, something . . . 'with a glamour to it, a perfection, a symmetry like Grecian art.'" One can almost see it: the imposing plantation homes, the gracious belles and cultured gentlemen, the picturesque black mammies, the carefree darkies at their tasks, laboring cheerfully, singing their melodious songs after a day of frolicing in the fields.

Whatever comfort and inspiration the white South was able to find in the aftermath of the Civil War seemed in many ways confined to an evocation, a celebration of the past, to an elaboration of myths about the "Old South" and the "lost cause." Even when faced with the enormous challenge of reconstruction, few Southern whites cared to subject their social order and racial relationships to a critical examination. The kinds of questions they chose to ask about the future revealed only a grim determination to recover the past—to find new ways of exploiting black labor and black lives. "Can not freedmen be organized and disciplined as well as slaves? Is not the dollar as potent as the lash? The belly as tender as the back?" Obsessed with the "lost cause," alarmed over the consequences of emancipation, all too many whites, no matter what social class they occupied, vented their frustration and anger upon the newly freed slaves. How many black men and women were beaten, flogged, mutilated, and murdered in the first years of freedom will never be known. Nor could any body count reveal the barbaric savagery and depravity that characterized assaults on the freedmen in the name of restraining their savagery and depravity—the severed ears and entrails, the mutilated sex organs, the burnings at the stake, the forced drownings, the open display of skulls and severed limbs as trophies. The white South, if it responded at all to the atrocities, chose to recall how slavery had afforded black men and women a positive protection from such violence.

The victorious North seemed as ill prepared to undertake a serious reconstruction of Southern society. It approached the task very much divided over the place of free black men and women in their own society. There is little reason to question the estimate of W. E. B. DuBois that at the outset of the Civil War probably not one white American in one hundred believed that Negroes could become an integral part of American democracy. Nor did that proportion change significantly during the war. No less a devoted abolitionist than George Julian had to concede to his Indiana constituents in 1865, "The real trouble is that we hate the Negro. It is not his ignorance that offends us, but his color." It was in this context that the North would make its commitment to black suffrage and civil rights. And it was in this context that newly freed black men and women in the South would seek to define their freedom. "The Master he says we are all free," George King recalled, "but it don't mean we is white. And it don't mean we is equal. Just equal for to work and earn our own living and not depend on him for no more meats and clothes."

With the passage of time, black men and women who had endured enslavement came to articulate a disillusionment that encompassed both their bondage and the tortured freedom they had enjoyed since emancipation. Patsy Mitchner was about 12-years-old when the Yankees passed through North Carolina. She fled, along with the other slaves on the plantation, and settled in a nearby town. "I have worked for white folks, washin', cookin', and wurkin' at a laundry ever since freedom come." Some seventy years after emancipation, when interviewed about her life, she had no reason to recall her bondage with any nostalgia. Her master had treated the blacks "mean," she had seen her mother beaten, the food, clothing, and sleeping quarters had been "bad," and her mother, brother, and sister had been sold to a slave speculator and shipped to Mississippi "in a box-car." Reflecting on her enslavement and quasi-freedom, she could talk only of different degrees of oppression.

> Slavery wus a bad thing an' freedom, of de kin' we got wid nothin' to live on wus bad. Two snakes full of pisen. One lyin' wid his head pintin' north, de other wid his head pintin' south. Dere names wus slavery an' freedom. De snake called slavery lay wid his head pinted south an' de snake called freedom lay with his head pinted north. Both bit de nigger, an' dey wus both bad.

What Patsy Mitchner suggested, the experience of four million black men and women after the Civil War confirmed: emancipation introduced still other forms of white duplicity and coercion, the attitudes and behavior which had justified and underscored enslavement persisted in different guises, and the theory of Negro inferiority blunted the North's commitment to racial equality even as it shaped the white South's response to the brief post-war experiment in bi-racial democracy. The dominant society refused to rearrange its values, priorities, and deeply held beliefs to grant to black Americans a positive assistance commensurate with the inequalities they had suffered and the magnitude of the problems they faced. More than a century of black freedom has not significantly altered Patsy Mitchner's assessment, only sharpened it, only deepened its tragic implications, only underscored the terrible paradox of black men and women attempting to achieve economic and political equality in a society which viewed such efforts as futile for an inferior race and feared any evidence to the contrary.

For black Americans, there appeared to be no way to assimilate, no way to separate, and most of the time most of them tried to suck what joy they could out of a bad situation. With the normal outlets for protest often closed, it was left ultimately to the bluesman to give the fullest expression to the unfairness blacks sensed about their lives.

> Well, I drink to keep from worrying and I laugh to keep from
> crying, (twice)
> I keep a smile on my face so the public won't know my mind.
> Some people thinks I am happy but they sho' don't know my
> mind, (twice)
> They see this smile on my face, but my heart is bleeding all the
> time.

Did the Confederacy Change Southern Soldiers? Some Obvious and Some Unobtrusive Measures

MICHAEL BARTON

Is it true, as Emory Thomas has written, that "the Confederate experience affected the Southern mind to such a degree as to create a Confederate mind?" Did Southerns find their "individualism circumscribed" and their "provincialism eroded" at the end of the war? Did the war create a "Confederate identity" which was a "modification of the Southern self-concept?"[1] In particular, did all those things happen to Southern soldiers as they fought their war?

I am not qualified to comment on all the features of Thomas's rich findings in *The Confederate Nation* and *The Confederacy as a Revolutionary Experience* because I am not a Civil War historian. I do historical psychological anthropology. I try to study the American character systematically. My published work happens to concern Civil War soldiers mainly because so many questions about national character come to a head in the scholarship on the Civil War, and because Civil War soldiers happened to create a remarkable pool of personal documents to use in national character study.[2] In any case, I am eager to comment on Thomas's conclusions about changes in Southern identity and self-concept because that is one feature of his work that fits with mine.

Talk about identity and self-concept is talk about the psychology of personality. Erik Erikson, the most excellent and sensitive student of psychosocial identity, cites William James and puts it this way: A person who finds his identity exclaims, "*This* is the real me."[3] It can be the case that men will find their identities in the act of committing themselves to something much larger than themselves. Erikson was not the first to notice this irony. St. Francis prayed that "It is in giving that we receive; it is in pardoning that we are pardoned; and it is in dying that we are born to eternal life." And St. Francis was only glossing what Jesus had preached, that "whosoever will lose his life for my sake shall find it." Civil War soldiers had the chance to commit themselves to something considerably larger than themselves, and this should give us a change to see them expressing their identities. In the roughest possible sense of these two words, war is a laboratory or an experiment for studying identity processes. It is an instance of what Bruno Bettelheim has called behavior in extreme situations.[4]

But there is one warning that must be posted about identity in general before we study it. Some psychologists believe there may be no such thing as a stable or reliable identity in a person now or in the past. Kenneth Gergen, for example, has found that depending on how you manipulate a subject just before he takes a test on identity, you can watch his scores flip-flop. If you put a subject into a situation that makes him feel bad about himself just before he is tested, then his identity score will not look very good on the test. And if you make him feel good about himself before you test him, then his identity score will be better. In other words, Gergen says identity is highly plastic and specific.[5] Of course, other researchers disagree. This is not the place to describe all the research and the debates about identity, but it is useful to know that historians have handled the idea of identity more confidently than it probably deserves to be. Talk about the identities of Northerners and Southerners and how they changed or stayed the same during the Civil War may amount to little but talk, from a hard-nosed psychologist's point of view.

The remains of Civil War soldiers' identities are in their wartime diaries and letters. I have chosen to study diaries here because they provide us with a precise chronological record of verbal behavior and with revelations of identity that we can date. In short, they give us truly historical descriptions of individual lives. Diaries can be an accounting of men talking to themselves about themselves. The trouble with diaries is, that's usually not their main purpose. Diaries are full of answers to questions that the diarists asked themselves, not questions that we would have asked them. Civil War diarists wanted to record external events more often than they wanted to chart their internal lives. But there is still enough overt and covert self-revelation in Civil War diaries for us to call them useful. They are usually spontaneous, private documents, and that makes them especially useful. Diaries usually do not try to explain events or their authors to someone else, and that distinguishes them from letters. Revelations in letters, of course, can be very useful, but revelations in letters are shaped by role requirements, which is to say that when Sgt. Doyle writes to Mother Doyle, he probably writes as her son and not necessarily as just himself. Role behavior is part of the self, of course, but in this case I am after revelations which are less alloyed. Memoirs and autobiographies are even trickier documents in this respect because therein Sgt. Doyle is explaining himself to the public. This is not to say that such documents are a pack of lies, but they are surely a pack of presentations of the self, which are not the same as private revelations.[6] Memoirs and autobiographies have the advantage, and disadvantage, of hindsight and reflection, and these qualities too are facets of the self. But public personal documents are not the same as the spontaneous record written on the spot. If we want to study a man's identity or self-concept in the 1860s, we would do well to study what he wrote in the 1860s and not what he wrote in the 1890s. There is no such thing as "pure" self-revelation, not even in the confessional; moreover, some students of the diary have asserted that every diarist has in mind some imaginary reader, whether he stores his record in a trunk or hands it to his family after the war as a sort of collection of belated letters. But diaries are still the most authentic "personal" documents we can get. Of course, I would like to have interviewed all these diarists, and even given them psychological tests and questionnaries, but those can be deceiving sources too, again, because the subject knows that he is performing for someone else a task that he did not invent himself. Diaries are inventions of the self, for the self, and that's their power. Incidently, all this is more commonsense than it is psychological science; the few psychologists who have studied diaries have not told us much more than this.[7]

One way to use diaries in historical research on identities is to pick out all the "good" diaries first, then pick out all the "good" quotations from the "good" diaries, and then tie them all together in a remarkably eloquent and omniscient narrative. I am certain this can be an effective strategy rhetorically and just as sure it can be wrong-headed systematically. That strategy ignores the "bad," uninteresting diaries which are, nevertheless, valid evidence from members of a culture. That strategy may take quotations out of context, but, worse yet, it may ignore the whole stream of entries in any one diary. And that strategy makes all the diaries appear, in summary, more coherent than they usually are. Indeed, our general policy in history of telling stories about populations—artful generalizations we call them—is always trouble-filled at best, from a systematic point of view. (Of course, systematic history is full of its own troubles too.) Another way to put it is to say that the problem with narrative history is that the narrative just may not be there, except in the study of some very limited political, military, or diplomatic events.[8] All history is interpretation, of course. If we really tried to let the data speak for themselves we would find the facts mute and our readers gone. But some interpretations based on the general story-telling strategy run that risk constantly. They assume more control over all the collected and uncollected evidence than historians usually have or probably can have. I can hardly solve this problem here, but at least I will try to avoid running into it. I will not tell a story about all Southerners' identities.

Now I will describe what I have done with Confederate diaries in order to test Thomas's claims about changes in Southern identities. I chose two tactics: First, I looked for the obvious evidence and described it, and then I sorted and counted it, and, second, I looked for the unobtrusive evidence and then I sorted and counted it. Sorting documentary evidence and then counting it some people call "content analysis." I consider it simply a more exacting and tedius form of note-taking and summarizing. Most historians practice content analysis anyway when they read a stack of documents, but where they would give the essence (one hopes) of the documents in an example, I will finally offer a number. In this case the obvious evidence lies in the clear remarks soldiers made about their allegiances; the unobtrusive evidence lies in the writing habits of the men, habits which I take to be the less than conscious revelations of their identities.[9]

Here are the details of the first tactic. I read seventy-two published Confederate diaries, 42 by Southern officers and 30 by enlisted Southerners. Not all of them were "good," interesting diaries. Indeed, I can not imagine why some of them were published, because they are perfectly boring and uninformative. Journal editors were probably just publishing many of them as "fillers" during the Civil War centenniel. But the mixture of good, bad, and mediocre diaries (I had planned it that way) served to deflect the criticism that my sample of published diaries is bound to be different from the universe of unpublished diaries. I used published diaries because they are full of biographical data about their authors. I could unfold nearly 400 pages of computer printout that breakdown all the characteristics of my sample, but let it suffice to say that these diarists were much like ordinary confederate soldiers with one exception: they were unusually well-educated. In fact, about 60 percent were either college students or graduates, or else they were in the midst of, or had completed, legal or medical studies.[10] The most obvious explanation for this bias would seem to be that highly educated soldiers were likely to write diaries and to have highly educated descendants who would want to see to it that their ancestors' personal documents got published. Whatever the explanation, I go to some length in my book to demonstrate that highly educated diarists did not differ significantly from less educated diarists in the values they expressed or in certain significant writing habits.[11] My point is, the sample's bias in favor of high education is an interesting fact but not necessarily a poisonous one for this kind or research. If I am wrong, if high education really does affect my results, then I will retreat to a defense that cultural anthropologists sometimes offer for picking the most articulate natives to be their informatives in field work. Anthropologists will say that the best and brightest informants are, indeed, a "biased" sample of the tribe, but that does not necessarily make them a bad sample, for they may provide the most insightful observations on other members of the tribe. So I submit that either my highly educated diarists do not affect my results at all or else they improve them. I admit that sounds like heads-I-win-tails-you-lose, but, in any case, we know the direction of the bias, if there is one.

Here are a few descriptions of the obvious evidence, examples of what the diarists had to say about their identities. By identity incidentally, I mean whether they saw themselves as individuals, as Southerners, or as something combined, or as something in between.

The opening and closing entries of the diaries may often disclose the soldier's primary identification. Officer James E. Hall began his diary in May, 1861 with the sentence, "I have volunteered in the Confederate Army" (p. 11). He does not mention his state, regiment, or country until later; he wrote of his Confederate nationality first of all. How did he end his diary? On April 28, 1865, he simply wrote, "went fishing" (p. 139). In the fourth entry in his diary on September 10, 1862, Maj. James McCreary wrote that "All seemed determined to throw off the Northern yoke and make ourselves the fairest, best, most glorious free country in the world" (p. 98). At the beginning of his diary in

September, 1863, Capt. Joseph Wescoat reflected on the significance of Ft. Sumter. Its capture by the South, he said, was "the first victorious offering of South Carolina to the Confederacy" (p. 14). Near the end of his diary in April, 1865, he wrote that he was sad to see that "our officers, Confederate officers, should give up now after sacrificing so many lives" (p. 94). In his last entry on April 30, while a prisoner of war, Wescoat proclaimed that he would not take the oath of loyalty to the United States: "Some brave fellows have swallowed the pap—but it shall never be said that J. J. Wescoat was recreant to his country." (p. 95). In Capt. J. J. Womack's first entry, dated May 16, 1861, he wrote of the "seceded states" becoming an "independent government" (p. 1), and in his last entry, dated December 31, 1863, he wrote, "Thus ends the year of our Lord, one thousand eight hundred and sixty three; and of American Independence the eighty seventh; and of the great American rebellion the third" (p. 115). Pvt. William Chambers, in the first sentence of his first entry on March 25, 1863, wrote "This morning I left the home of my parents to become a unit in the army of the South," (p. 227). In his sixth entry of March 20, 1862, Corp. Edmund Patterson, a former Northerner, wrote, "Now I am a soldier in the army of the Confederate states, and 'I am become a stranger unto my brethren and an alien unto my mother's children.' But I am engaged in the glorious cause of liberty and justice, fighting for the rights of man—fighting for all that we of the South hold dear" (p. 14). Lt. Albert Moses Luria closed his diary in January, 1862 with the proclamation, "long life and prosperity to the Southern Confederacy, and the same for our first President, Jefferson Davis!!!" (p. 103).

The entries that soldiers made on the Fourth of July are sometimes good spots to find Confederate nationalism expressed. Corp. J. G. Law wrote on July 4, 1861, "How different the celebration this anniversary of American Independence from any that have preceeded it. Now it is celebrated by the South on the tented field and by the North, by the assembling of the remnant of our National Congress to devise means for subjugation of the brave and independent people, who have risen in the might and thrown off the yoke of a corrupt and oppressive government hostile to our institutions and totally at variance with Southern customs and manners. So ended our first Confederate Fourth of July" (pp. 565–566). On the Fourth of July, 1862, Col. Randal McGavock wrote, "This is the anniversary of the independence of the U. S. Altho not a citizen of the U. S. now, yet I feel that we of the South are more entitled to celebrate and hold sacred the day than the people of the North. The declaration was the product of Southern mind, and it was for the principles contained in that instrument that induced me to take arms" (p. 647).

Other dates that could trigger a remark about Confederate nationalism included the anniversary of the opening shot at Ft. Sumter, the diarist's birthday, and the first day of the new year.

Not all diarists were clear-cut about their identity, of course; some played it two or three ways. Pvt. Louis Leon wrote on June 10, 1861, that he had taken up arms for "the old North State," meaning North Carolina, but at the end of the same entry he mentioned that he had built a bed, "fit for a King or a Confederate soldier" (pp. 4–5). On May 20, 1864, he split his sentiments again: "Three years ago today, the Old North State left the Union, and we went to the front full of hopes to speedily show the Yankee government that the South had a right to leave the Union" (p. 64). Lt. Richard Gray, a Virginian, spoke of other Virginians with him in prison and noted that at one dinner table there were nine persons: "4 states are represented and 2 nations" (p. 31). But returning home, Gray was relieved to discover that "we are among friends in Dixie", and he spoke of himself as one of the "thousands of sons of the South" (pp. 40–41). A perfect symbol of the sometime alliance of state and Confederate patriotism is found in the diary of Sgt. W. H. Andrews, who noted on July 17, 1861, that his regiment, the 1st Georgia Regulars, was "presented with a magnificent state and Confederate flag combined, by Miss Howard of Columbus, Georgia" (p. 2).

It is possible to go on quoting entries like these for some time. There is evidence in these diaries that some Southeners developed a Confederate identity over and above, or at least in addition to, their local identities during the war. Soldiers asserted that nearly everyone else was developing a Confederate identity too. Corp. Edmund Patterson wrote about a nurse, Mrs. Quarles, who saved his life: "It mattered not that object of her care be unknown to her; she knows them to be soldiers of our Sunny South. She does it all for the South. And there are many others like her" (pp. 37–38). Randal McGavock remarked while in prison on the unifying effects of the war: "This Revolution," he wrote, "has brought about a strange state of things. Men of all denominations in the South have been brought together in one common brotherhood" (p. 630). You do not test a theory adequately, however, just by finding support for it; you have to try to get a theory into trouble when you test it. You have to put it into "maximum jeopardy," as one theorist said.

But how can we put Thomas's theory into jeopardy? Can we find any remarks which contradict the ones noted so far? As a matter of record, I have not found anyone who wrote, "I have not become a Confederate." There is evidence suggesting that some Southern soldiers still had local identities. Lt. Rufus Woolwine, for example, appeared to have little interest in the Confederacy during the time he kept his diary from July, 1861, to June, 1865. At the end he only hopes that "we may again place our dear old state on her original high standing" (p. 448). Some soldiers don't mention the Confederacy, the South, or their locality at all. They simply tell you where they marched, what they ate, and who they fought. Therefore, as I see it, the only systematic way to test Thomas's theory, if not jeopardize it, is to keep track of how many men, across time, seemed to express Confederate identities, how many seemed to express more local identities, and how many seemed to express only their individual identities. Therefore, I went back to the diaries and chose one day at random from every month from January, 1861, to December, 1865.

Then I read the entries for those days again in the diaries and summarized with a code number what seemed to be the focus of identity in those entries. Of course, not every diary had an entry for August 28, 1863, for example, so I often had to take the date that was closest. Also, only a few of the diaries were longer than two or three years; some were only a few months. The average diary length was about one year, so most of my measurements are not as longitudinal as they ought to be for a good test. But at least this gives us a series of somewhat experimental conditions.

If a soldier only mentioned himself, I coded him for self-identity. If he wrote only about his military unit, I coded him for unit identity, whether it was his entire regiment or just a few of his comrades that he mentioned. If he only wrote about the South or the Confederacy, I coded him for Confederate identity. Of course, as I have already demonstrated, some soldiers would talk about themselves, their military units, and the Confederacy all at the same time in the same entry, so I devised four other codes for self and unit, unit and Confederacy, self, unit, and Confederacy, and self and Confederacy. Finally, if a soldier just wrote "rained today" or "marched five miles," I coded him for no explicit identity expressed, since you cannot tell in those entries whether he is thinking about himself, his unit, or the whole South. Only about 10 percent of the entries, however, had no explicit identity expressed in them.

I had hoped to be able to compare all the identity rates year by year, but some of the years simply did not provide enought data, and some of the codes simply were not used very often, so I went back to my charts and collapsed them; that is, I split my random entries into two halves, the first half covering January 1861, to the end of June, 1863, and the second half from July, 1863, to December, 1865. Then I split my codes down the middle, comparing those entries which mentioned either self only, self and unit, or unit only, with those entries which mentioned either unit and Confederacy, self and Confederacy, self, unit, and Confederacy, or Confederacy alone. These two changes let me compare diary entries from the first half of the war with those from the second half of the war, and identity statements that mention the Confederacy with those that do not. In the re-coding I simply ignored those entries that did not express any identities.

In my final analysis, I still had 72 Confederate diaries, 42 from Southern officers and 30 from enlisted Southerners. I had a total of 694 coded entries, 412 in the first half of the war and 282 in the last half. There were 203 coded entries from Southern officers in the first half and 177 in the last half. There were 209 entries from enlisted men in the first half, and 105 in the last half.

The patterns of identity rates I found are remarkably regular. In the first half of the war, 83 percent of the diary entries are about the men themselves or their units; only 17 percent mention the Confederacy. In the second half of the war the ratio is *exactly* the same: 83 percent of the entries are about the men themselves or their units; only 17 percent mention the Confederacy. Considering all the soldiers, there is no change in the focus of identity in the diaries I have studied. Looking at my data from another angle, about 59 percent of the "self" or "local" identity remarks are found in the first half of the war, and 41 percent in the last half. And the percentages of "Confederate" identity remarks are, again, exactly the same—59 percent are in the first half, 41 percent are in the second half of the war. I have never found results in my ten years of research on Civil War soldiers which are so perfectly undifferentiated as these. What also surprised me is that there were no significant differences between the identity rates of Southern officers and enlisted men. Among Southern officers, 84 percent of the entries in the first half of their diaries focus on self or local unit, versus 81 percent in the second half. Among enlisted Southerners 82 percent of the entries in the first half are coded self or local, versus 86 percent in the second half.

Of course, these results hardly close the case against Thomas's thesis. One could argue that even if the rate of identification with the Confederacy did not change throughout the Civil War, it is

still significant that 17 percent of diary entries mention the Confederacy, or the Sunny South, or Dixie, or whatever. Perhaps
that figure is high enough to lend support to his thesis. I did not
try   to   scale   changes   in   the   *intensity*   of   Confederate
identifications, and that is a shortcoming. One could also fault the
research by saying that a fair and proper test would have used
diaries that began long before the war and ended long after the
war, so that we might find out if Confederate identification was
lower than 17 percent before the war and higher than 17 percent
after the war. Those dates are probably the real boundaries of
Thomas's thesis. I would look forward to seeing the results of
such a test, but I doubt that one can easily find enough Southern
diaries that cover so much time, including service in the war. I
found that the beginning of the war started most of the diaries
written during the Middle Period and that the end of the war
stopped most of them. I would also add that if I were to do this
study again with many more diaries, I would distinguish between
entries which mentioned the Confederate government and those
which mentioned the Southern way of life.

I performed a second test on the less than conscious writing
habits of the men. The first test isolated references to the Confederacy; this second test runs the opposite direction and isolates
references to the self. But while the first test judged entire entries, the second test counts only a part of speech: pronouns.

The rationale for this test is straight-forward: I claim that if a
man's identity is mainly individualistic, then he will usually write
"I," "me," "my," "myself," or "mine" when he has the chance to
use a pronoun in a diary entry. I call these ego pronouns. Con-
versely, if a man's identity has a larger orbit than the self—if he
identifies with his friends, his unit, or his culture—then I claim
he will more often write "we," "us," "ourselves," and so on, when
he has the chance to use a pronoun in his diary. I call these
solidarity pronouns. This method has some precedent in psychology, if not in history. Research on the changing language patterns
of people who go through psychotherapy lends support to my

claim.[12] There is also an excellent and famous essay by Roger Brown, which shows how power relations between persons are systematically revealed by their use of particular pronouns and forms of address.[13] But I think one will see this method as either credible on its face or not.

For this tactic I had to handle the diaries differently. Rather than divide the span of the war in half, I divided each diary in half. I took ten entries at random from each half. I then counted the number of ego and solidarity pronouns in each entry. If ego pronouns dominated, I treated that entry as one simple win for ego; if solidarity pronouns outnumbered ego pronouns, I treated that entry as one simple win for solidarity. For each half of each diary, then, I had three scores: The number of ego wins, the number of solidarity wins, and the number of ties. Then I could compare the three scores in the first half with the three scores in the last half in each diary and see if each type of pronoun increased, decreased, or remained constant. For this tactic I had a total of 52 diaries, 26 each from Southern officers and enlisted men.

If my first tactic, the content analysis, was trustworthy, and if this second tactic, the pronoun analysis, is theoretically sound, then the results of both tests should agree. They do. I find no significant changes in pronoun usage when I compare the 520 entries in the first halves of the diaries with the 520 entries in the second halves. Again, there is remarkable consistency.

Considering all the soldiers and the first halves of their diaries, 26 percent of the entries had ego pronouns dominating solidarity pronouns, 34 percent had solidarity pronouns dominating ego pronouns, and 40 percent of the entries had both types of pronouns tied. The reason so many entries were tied is because almost half the time there were no pronouns at all in the entries—it was a nothing-to-nothing tie. Considering all the soldiers and the second halves of their diaries, the percentage of entries in which ego dominates solidarity stayed *exactly* the same as it was in the first halves—26 percent. The percentage of ties in the second halves goes down slightly, from 40 percent to 38 percent, and the percentage of entries in which solidarity dominates ego goes up slightly, from 34 percent to 36 percent.

When we divide the soldiers according to their military rank, again the differences between Southern officers and enlisted men are not significant. Enlisted men use slightly more ego pronouns than their officers do, but they also use slightly more solidarity pronouns. And again, in both groups of soldiers, there is no more than a 1 percent change in any pronoun score when first half entries are compared with second half entries. In general, about a third of the soldiers were more likely to say, for example, "We" than "I" and about a fourth were more likely to say, "I" than "We," but they did not often switch from one type of pronoun to another. If we count heads, we find that only 6 out of 52 soldiers switched from ego to solidarity pronoun domination in the second half. Perhaps their "provincialism was eroded." But just about as many soldiers (5 out of 52) switched from solidarity to ego domination in the second half. Their individualism seems to have been released, not "circumscribed." More than half of the soldiers (28 out of 52) maintained their type of pronoun dominance, whichever it was, throughout their diaries, and the remainder (13 out of 52) had ties either in their first or second half and thus there was no clear switch.

One of the same criticisms that could be directed at the first tactic in my research could be directed against this second tactic; that is, I have only checked pronoun rates in diaries written in the war. Also, I admit that this kind of analysis treats, for example, all uses of "I" as having the same weight, even though the diarist might have thought that some of his "I's" were more important than other "I's."

In summary, my limited research on direct and indirect expressions of identity in Southern soldiers' diaries does not support Emory Thomas's thesis that the Confederate experience modified Southerner's self-concepts, as I defined them operationally. His thesis is surely plausible and deliciously ironic—it's just the sort of thing you'd like to find out about the fate of true believers. But I find instead that their expressions of identity were remarkably stable throughout the Civil War.

Let me close with some other qualifications. First, I know I work not with fine scalpels but with blunt instruments, and that perhaps I should be arrested for having bludgeoned these intimate diaries. I want sharper tools, but at least these cannot be concealed and are easily reported if wrongly used. I believe it was Allan Nevins who said historians ought to labor vigorously in their research but then try just as hard to hide that labor in their writing. The trouble with that dictum, of course, is that readers cannot then argue about the quality of your labor. Moreover, blunt instruments may be the best ones to use if we want a general answer to a general question, and that is what I have tried to ask and answer here.

Finally, I want to plead that the end of history is not just to describe people or, God forbid, count them. As my advisor, Michael Zuckerman, once wrote, our purpose is to show men and women not only what they have *been*, but also what they can *become*, because that is their most historic quality of all.

The Dimensions of
Continuity
Across the Civil War

THOMAS B. ALEXANDER

The breadth of our concern these three days has been made
evident to anyone who did not already recognize how intercon-
nected all of Southern history is and how little of it can be
disassociated from the Civil War. Your symposium coordinator
wrote to me last spring that "fundamentally, we are asking if the
Civil War ended the Old South, or whether significant characteristics of the Old South survived the Confederacy." "If the latter
be indicated," he continued, "we should ask when did the Old
South come to an end?" Then, in informing me that I would
appear last, he casually slipped in the notion that I would therefore be summarizing parts of the continuity debate and have
opportunity to point new directions. Now, it seems too embar-
rassingly obvious to mention that the lack of agreement on what
constituted the essence of the Old South is a handicap when
trying to weigh continuity versus change of that essence. On the
other hand, let me hasten to confess that the professor who
taught my sophomore sociology class warned me that I would
never understand people because I took too logical an approach.
I have struggled ever since to become less logical, but I am still
unable tonight to see any ready path around the pitfall of absence
of consensus on what the Old South really was.

It does not take one long to discover that not only is consensus
lacking about the essence of Southernism but that one line of
argument denies the existence of anything uniquely Southern

and concedes only that Southern traits were exceptional, if at all, in being slight exaggerations of American traits. As for the impact of war on the course of history, it seems that almost every interpreter with an ideological ax to grind has seized upon the Civil War as a cardinal example of—needless to say—all kinds of incompatible effects. Postwar developments are treated as falling anywhere between one extreme of being dictated absolutely by war consequences to the other extreme of being perfectly predictable trends along a secular-change current that was hardly rippled by the war. Elaborate efforts to define the Old South continue to appear, and David Potter made a characteristically rapier-thrust comment in a review essay of Simkins' *The Everlasting South* and the symposium, edited by Frank Vandiver, *The Idea of the South: Pursuit of a Central Theme*. Potter suggested that some are more concerned with telling us where to go to find Southern identity than with telling us what it is. He concluded that 1964 essay with his prediction that the quest for a central theme would continue, for, as he wrote, "the South remains as challenging as it is baffling, which is about as challenging as a subject can be."[1]

I have been led into considerable previously unplanned reading since last spring and have been recalling with increasing clarity one of Thor's experiences according to Teutonic legend. In the castle of a king of magic, Thor humiliatingly failed one test after another of his legendary strength. The final test was merely to pick up a cat sitting nearby, but the best he could do was to get one of the cat's paws off the floor momentarily. The following morning Thor's host took pity enough to explain to him that all the failures had been brought about by magic. The cat, for instance, was actually a segment of the serpent of Midgard, whose coils surround the earth itself, and when Thor had lifted even one paw, earthquakes had shaken the world.

The Old South in the Crucible of War may have seemed manageable enough, but its coils encompass the whole of Southern history. I respectfully request to be excused from trying to pick up that cat; but as a guest of such gracious hosts it would be rude of me not to at least rub its ears a bit and try to evoke a purr or two. I shall not entirely shirk the invitation to summarize some portion of the continuity debate and to make a few modest suggestions about promising directions to look for further insights. First, however, I propose to comment on several studies that share a common theme: the perceptions of many of the Southern elite during the first few years after the Civil War about the extent of change and continuity. It is not necessarily the case that their perceptions were valid, or if valid more than superficial. But since we are still trying to get the real South to materialize so that all can see, it should do no harm to observe the actors in the postwar drama. Much, though not all, of this line of investigation falls generally within the purview of political history, and that seems to call for a caveat.

Political history has fallen into disrepute in recent years. In an ambitious symposium on "The New History: The 1980s and Beyond," a symposium almost filling the most recent two issues of the *Journal of Interdisciplinary History*, one of the contributors comments on some current outright rejection of politics as ineffective and irrelevant. Such rejectionists argue that "Whatever statesmen do or say . . . turbulent upheavals, even revolutions, lead to false illusions: they, too, end up perpetuating continuities." "Socioeconomic structures endure, in this view, and common people fashion strategies for survival and self-protection in recognition of this simple principle. It is on this humble level that one can glimpse the dignity of struggle, and it is here, in daily tests of endurance, that we can best observe the drama of humanity's predicament."[2] This phrasing by Peter H. Smith, who nevertheless endorses the relevance of political history, seems poignantly appropriate in remembering the mass of ordinary Southerners, white or black. Almost all of my colleagues in this symposium have very recently made such distinguished contributions, directly or indirectly, to our capacity to empathize in that "drama of humanity's predicament" across the Civil War years, and brought so much of their illuminating perceptions to us in these three days, that I have no real qualms about turning briefly to elite history and even to political elites.

I have long been interested in the behavior of white Southerners during the interval between defeat of the Confederate efforts and the imposition of certain political constraints by the national Congress in 1867—the period of Presidential Reconstruction. My own observations of the surviving record suggest a pervasive assumption on the part of white Southerners seeking to retain positions of power that restoration, not change from the old ways, was the obvious goal. My work on Tennessee convinced me that the postwar political history of that state was essentially dictated by identifiable considerations from the Old South years: intrastate sectionalism, antebellum party antagonism that almost paralleled wartime animosities, and the indelible imprint of racial perceptions. I found, also, that continuity of political leadership across the war years was overwhelmingly the rule. Looking farther than Tennessee, I found that the immediate postwar political landscape was simply dominated by rivalry between prewar Unionists and Immediate Secessionists, a rivalry that in many parts of the South amounted nearly to the old familiar antebellum two-party politics, Whigs against Democrats. I would not want to generalize about the entire South from what Sydney Andrews wrote while traveling through North Carolina in 1866, yet the implications may not be far from the mark for much of the region. Andrews wrote: ". . . here, in North Carolina, I discover, with proper amazement, that the old parties are both alive, and neither of them a whit older or less pugilistic than it was twenty years ago. . . ."[3] It is more than coincidence that in the 1865 congressional elections in the nine former Confederate states where the Whig party had had respectable antebellum organizations, old Whigs were elected to almost nine tenths of the United States House seats. In the Tennessee legislature elected in 1865, former Whigs held almost one hundred of the 109 seats. All but one member of the Virginia House of

Delegates were formerly Whigs. And throughout the region Whigs and Douglas Democrats of 1860 dominated the elective offices.[4] The dimension of continuity is, of course, the two-party rivalry as modified by the Unionist-Secessionist axis.

When by 1866 it became apparent that President Andrew Johnson's program was in trouble in the North and the widely publicized National Union Convention was called to meet in Philadelphia to support Johnson, the Southern way of claiming white solidarity against Republican party proposals for a different kind of political reconstruction was to send to Philadelphia state delegations that were either ostentatiously bipartisan or consisted overwhelmingly of those who had been Unionists in the secession crisis. Both kinds of delegations reflected the antebellum political landscape, though in different ways. Earlene Collier in studying the Southern delegates discovered that they were preponderantly antebellum political leaders and that many had been Confederate officials.[5]

Linking the records of individual political officeholders from antebellum into postbellum years is tedious and time-consuming work, made almost immeasurably more troublesome by incorporating in the study the unsuccessful candidates for political office. Among the few state studies that provide massive documentation of continuity of individual political participation across the Civil War years would certainly be included the prodigious labors of William C. Harris on Mississippi and William M. Cash, Jr., on Alabama.[6] Their success in tracing many hundreds of individuals, taken together with much fine work on other states, makes abundantly clear the continuity of a Southern political elite from antebellum to postbellum years. The recent volume on Alabama Black Belt planters by Jonathan Wiener emphasizes from individual-level analysis the extent of planter-family continuity in that part of Alabama, and numerous recent studies have at least tangentially offered further support to the widely held view that landowning dominance went through no revolutionary process because of the war.[7] Twenty-five years ago J. Carlyle Sitterson reported from a study of 120 nonagricultural business leaders in North Carolina that being born into families of considerable substance in the antebellum period was characteristic of the great majority of successful business men after the war. He uncovered, moreover, a remarkable amount of actual family and in-law continuity in the same kind of business enterprise spanning the war years.[8]

Three extensive studies of the Deep South during the Presidential Reconstruction interval, when native white Southerners had relatively great freedom in managing adjustments to wartime impacts, tell essentially the same story. Harris's first book on Mississippi, after exploring many facets of the readjustment period, concludes that antebellum experience provided the frame of reference for postwar alignments. Fomer Whigs, as Unionists of 1860, seized the inside track in designing state policies; but, writes Harris, "In the end they followed policies more attuned to prewar experiences than those which fully recognized the harsh realities of postwar adjustment." Sylvia Krebs, addressing the same wide range of concerns, concludes: "The majority of white Alabamians were inclined to adhere to past experience and familiar principle unless forced to do otherwise by circumstances beyond their control. These people attempted to pick up the threads that had been raveled and broken by the war and to continue weaving the same life pattern. . . . Under these circumstances, restoration of a former way of life seemed far more likely than any decided innovation to produce a new society."[9] Westley F. Busbee, Jr., was convinced by his exhaustive study of Georgia's Presidential Reconstruction that a gloomy outlook for long-lasting accomplishments cannot be blamed primarily on intrusion by outsiders but that "the heaviest burden of failure must fall on the white people of Georgia." For "most whites," he concludes, "looked backward in time for solutions to new problems."[10]

The dimension of political continuity on into the period of Congressional Reconstruction of Alabama is documented heavily in a study that includes individual-level career information about twenty-seven hundred Alabama Republicans. William M. Cash reports that "Although some political newcomers were observed as officeholders, a pervasive characteristic of Republican participation . . . is continuity in officeholding from ante-bellum times through war and Presidential Reconstruction into the Congressional Reconstruction years. In addition, these Republicans did not differ radically in wealth, occupation, nativity, or age pattern from ante-bellum officeholders. . . ." Cash adds that almost all active Republicans among native-born white Alabamians had been Unionist in sentiment in 1860 and that the great bulk of Unionists away from the North Alabama hill country had been Whigs. "The inclination to Republicanism of these ante-bellum Alabama citizens," he notes, "evidently had roots in their ante-bellum experiences, loyalties, and attitudes." Acknowledging that many former Whigs and 1860 Unionists did not become Republicans, Cash maintains that "white Alabamians in Republican ranks did represent a line of succession characterized at each stage by opposition to Democratic party leaders and the policies of the dominant wing of the state Democratic party."[11] Social scientists studying voter behavior would characterize this as continuity of a negative reference group.

Vicki L. Vaughn has just completed a study of the Southern Commercial Conventions that brings strong corroborating evidence and considerable identification of the substance of continuity across the Civil War. Those convention sessions were held a score of times in a dozen Southern cities over a period of thirty-four years, from 1837 to 1871, involving almost eight thousand delegates. "As the convention moved from city to city in these years . . . the sessions as a whole . . . constitute a type of southwide regional assembly," she writes, providing the only "instance of a truly sectional body convening repeatedly over a long span of years." After thoroughgoing analysis of personal attributes of almost six thousand delegates, far more extensive assembling of data on the six hundred most active delegates, and close study of the content of all convention proceedings, the author has some well-buttressed conclusions relevant to the theme of our symposium.[12]

She establishes that leading delegates may properly be credited with legitimate elite status, writing:

> Individuals in the data set of this study portray many qualities that distinguish them as an elite within mid-nineteenth century southern society. . . . They held positions of real decision-making power as measured by their access to political offices of their state, federal, and Confederate governments. The shared social background which shaped their concept of a "good society" for the South provided the basis for a common group viewpoint. . . . The fact that six hundred of them were selected for positions of authority and honor at such non-politically oriented sessions as the conventions speaks further of the high regard in which they were held outside the limits of political officeholding. . . .

Turning to the perception this elite revealed in the course of convention debates before and after the Civil War, she summarizes those perceptions as follows:

> Their most consistent underlying conviction, both before and after the Civil War, was a firm optimism about the potential for southern economic growth. . . .
>
> If economic goals outlined at the prewar sessions are compared to those of the postwar sessions, similarities abound. . . . Sessions in neither time period looked to a revolution of the southern economy, to rapid or even widespread industrialization. The priority remained improvement of the agrarian sector of the economy. . . .
>
> Despite the wartime personal sufferings of the delegates themselves, or of their families and neighbors, they . . . brought to their discussions the same perceptions, schemes, and goals presented at prewar . . . conventions.

The personal characteristics of delegates participating in the postwar sessions from 1869 to 1871 proved to be the same as for the delegates attending conventions before the Civil War. Continuity of individuals was substantial, but continuity of attitudes and goals were so great as to be striking. The subtitle for this study of Southern Commerical Conventions is, surely appropriately, Continuity of Perceptions, Values, and Leadership, 1837–1871.

Why should white Southerners have been expected to entertain seriously anything but continuation of the familiar, apart from forcible emancipation? To all living Southerners of 1860 the region had been remarkably the same in essential respects for as long as they could remember. No inmigration of consequence, white or black had happened in living memory. The homogenizing consequences were reflected in the extent of religious uniformity across the region. Economic changes, while striking for places and for individuals as the Southern system rolled westward, were of the predictable kind, as the unfolding of petals of a familiar flower. The resulting contempt for reform zealots, more contempt than fear until the mid-fifties, flowed naturally from the plausible assumption that it if ain't broke, don't fix it. In probing the Southern mind on the eve of secession, Joel H. Silbey, in an essay appearing in the 1981 Walter Prescott Webb Memorial Lecutures, brilliantly describes the reactions of a self-satisfied people, with no sense of need for public meddling in private affairs, to a suddenly looming Republicanism they perceived as the very witches' brew of noxious, self-righteous extremism in America. With the war's disasters behind, why would such a society's leaders voluntarily consider innovation above restoration?

I did promise to rub the cat's ears a little, and it is time to turn to one ear. A third of a century ago, down the road a piece at Jackson, Mississippi, Robert S. Cotterill offered as his presidential address to the Southern Historical Association a comment on "The Old South to the New."[13] Here may be found the most extreme statement of the continuity theme. "In no phase of its economic life was the New South new," he announced. "It was not a Phoenix rising from the ashes of the Old; not a revival; not even a reincarnation: it was merely a continuation of the Old

South. And not only in its economic life: the New South inherited, also, the *spirit* of the Old. It inherited its racial pride, and if anyone wants to call it racial prejudice, there can be no objection. . . . The New South inherited, also, a laissez-faire philosphy of living . . . [and] the Old South conviction that certain questions could not be surrendered to the jurisdiction of public law." The Civil War, Cotterill claimed, "was, in long perspective, only an episode in a continuous southern history: a tragic episode, but even its tragedy was transient." And to make certain that no listener missed his point or retained composure if in disagreement, he concluded: "There is, in very fact, no Old South and no New. There is only The South. Fundamentally, as it was in the beginning it is now, and, if God please, it shall be evermore."

Well, that was a third of a century ago, and offered by a historian born about a century ago now. How has it seemed more recently? Two monumental studies of Reconstruction in individual states have recently appeared, Harris's on Mississippi and Joe Gray Taylor's on Louisiana.[14] Harris has, while exposing the baffling complexity of state affairs during Reconstruction, nonetheless provided a stunning body of evidence of old leadership and old ideas riding out some turbulent times to safe haven in familiar antebellum social and political arrangements. Professor Harris wrote to me this past summer about his residual impressions. So many of the prewar characteristics continued after the war, he thinks, that the main changes occurred as a result of the fact that the South had less of everything after the war, and that Southerners had to adjust their lives and institutions to this somber fact. Professor Taylor wrote to me that, in his opinion, the South for three quarters of a century after the Civil War was more like the antebellum South than like the South of the past four decades. Sharecropping was in some ways close to slavery, he thinks, and the plantation system continued with the same class though not necessarily the same people in control. Though white sharecropping was postbellum, Professor Taylor wonders what would have happened to the yeomen's surplus sons if there had been no war. He does not think that the growth of manufacturing made a significance difference because it was neither new nor substantial in any but a small part of the South. What finally ended the continuing South, in his judgment, was urbanization during and even after the Second World War.

What then of the South since the Second World War? Professor Charles P. Roland's recent fascinating volume on *The Improbable Era: The South Since World War II*, concludes with a chapter entitled "The Enduring South."[15] He describes what he considers to be objective differences that remain even today between the South and the rest of the nation, but he endorses the theme of an enduring South through a particular state of mind. "Recent scholarship suggests," he writes, "that the ultimate distinctiveness of the South may lie, not in its empirical dissimilarities from other regions, but in its unique mythology: those images of the region that give"—and here he quotes George Tindall—"'philosophical meaning to the ordinary facts of life.'" The parting shot of his book is to report that on the living room wall of a noted Southern advocate of racial desegregation and understanding hung a plaque of grateful recognition from the Detroit chapter of the NAACP, underneath which was displayed a pair of crossed Confederate rifles. Charlie Roland has not changed his mind very much during the past six years, as is clear from his presidential address to the Southern Historical Association in November 1981, entitled "The Ever-Vanishing South."[16]

Now, this is all very amusing gamesmanship, from Professor Cotterill to Professor Roland, we are saying to ourselves, but the truth is that one of even median age among us tonight knows that profound changes have come to the South, not only since the Civil War but in living memory. And then we are jolted to see a map of the United States showing where the proposed Equal Rights Amendment has not been ratified or where state legislatures have been making noises about rescinding their ratification. There, on the map, except for the splinter northeastern corner and the totally new world of the southwestern quarter still called by the old name, Texas, stands as solid a block of the 1860 slave states as ever enraged antebellum abolitionists. The obvious and common sense acknowledgment should easily follow. Of course there have been changes, and of course there are continuities. It is the dimensions of each that historians rightly continue to pursue.

The most profound change across the years of the Civil War was in the status of the black people of the South. In the company I am keeping this week, it does not behoove me to do more than refer to this dimension of significant change. I shall risk adding that to emphasize how frustrated the black people were at falling so far short of their hopes and their rights by calling the change in status not very significant is to carry escalated rhetoric much too far. A pair of items struck me this summer as carrying a heavy freight of the meaning of this change. In a 1785 estate settlement in Ste. Genevieve, in what is now Missouri, two slave mothers and two children were divided so as to establish as nearly as possible equal inheritance shares. Each slave mother of about thirty had a daughter of about twelve. By requiring the mothers to swap daughters, the estate shares were brought from 7 percent inequity in value to 3½ percent.[17] Decades after the Civil War, Jacob Thomas, who had seen his slave parents separated by sale, "had no difficulty in relating what for him had been the overriding significance of freedom." As reported by Professor Leon Litwack in his deeply moving recent book, *Been in the Storm So Long*, the aging Thomas replied: "I has got thirteen great-gran' chilluns an' I knows whar dey ever' one am."[18]

Those Southern families possessed of many slaves in 1860 surely went through what they perceived as devastating changes. James L. Roark's graceful portrayal of *Masters Without Slaves* concludes with a chapter entitled "The Soul is Fled."[19] While this judgment of the author ought to be seriously addressed in evaluating the dimensions of change, there is still room to question this aspect of his compelling account. In any case, the large slaveholders were such a tiny fraction of the Southern white families that only by making that affluent small minority surrogate for the essence of the Old South could such a devastating judgment be sustained. The great mass of white Southerners were, of course, not owners of any slaves, while many others used the labor of only one or two slaves. Recently Forrest McDonald and Grady McWhiney have been exploring the fate of these people in what they call in one essay "The South from Self-Sufficiency to Peonage."[20] Among the crucial elements in the decline, they identify the destruction of the great swine herds and the onset of legal requirements that herders fence in their stock. How much of these changes were already in the making, war or no war, and how much may be directly attributed to either war or emancipation remains to be studied.

This brings our attention to another of the self-evident changes across the war years, rural poverty replacing antebellum prosperity in agriculture. The difficulty of unraveling the effects of war itself from the less direct wartime influences as well as from secular trends only insignificantly deflected by the war has, however, been emphasized very recently by Gavin Wright's work on *The Political Economy of the Cotton South*. "The South was wrenched out of one historical epoch and into another during the decade of the Civil War," he writes. "True enough, the South had lost a bloody Civil War, but apart from the enforcement of emancipation, the changes in Southern agriculture were not imposed by a victorious North. . . ." "The suddenness and extent of the changes," he continues, "are explained instead by the unique historical justaposition of emancipation, war, and the onset of an era of stagnation in cotton demand." In further stressing the secular trend of market forces, Wright argues:

> The malaise of the postbellum South, the disputes and anxieties over tenancies, crop liens, interest charges, and overproduction, all confirm the rationality of the antebellum farmers who grew cotton only as a surplus crop. The behavior of these free households explains the demand for slave labor

and the flourishing success of slavery during the era when cotton was king. Postwar circumstances and institutions pushed farmers of both races toward the alternative rationality of the market, but the forces of market demand after 1860 were too weak to restore economic progress based on cotton.

It is therefore the worldwide weakening of demand for cotton, more than war related consequences, that Wright is emphasizing when he concludes: "Thus, not just slavery, but the self-sufficient prosperity of 1860, was gone with the wind forever."[21]

I am obligated to rub the cat's other ear at least briefly, so I shall now turn to pointing in some directions that if not necessarily new seem promising for further study of our symposium theme. The new history of the 1980s and beyond, so powerfully outlined in the 1981 Summer and Autumn issues of the *Journal of Interdisciplinary History,* offers many exciting vistas for the study of our central problem. Family history, for example, has currently become almost a rage, and where is there a more fruitful field for either traditional family history or family reconstitution than in an area where society is self-consciously organic and family is sometimes a mortal religion—a religion equipped with perhaps more genealogical ministers per thousand people than any place in America. The undeniable impact of a war such as the Civil War on family relations, sex roles, child rearing practices, remarriages, and step-parent influences on children await only better research techiques and organizing concepts to advance significantly our understanding of nineteenth-century American society.

The onset of the psychological perspective in biography, for another example, should be welcomed by biographers of Southerners if, indeed, the distinctiveness of the South lies in its unique mythology that gives "philosophical meaning to the ordinary facts of life." Professor Michael Barton's discovery that almost all of the published letters of condolence on the death of loved ones were written by Confederate rather than Federal soldiers during the Civil War is so intriguing that he may have to move fast to keep his investigations ahead of those of others he has stimulated to enter the lists.[22]

The psychological dimensions of a society are being approached repeatedly through study of the process of elite recruitment. Though it is woefully superficial to assess any society from the simple notion of "show me a peoples' heroes," serious comparison of antebellum with postbellum Southern society along this dimension may be possible. Johanna Nicol Shields offers suggestive insights into elite temperament and its roots in her study of "The Making of American Congressional Mavericks: A Contrasting of the Cultural Attitudes of Mavericks and Conformists in the United States House of Representatives, 1836–1860."[23] Anyone with the stamina to digest tens of thousands of pages of autobiographical and other self-revealing writings of postwar Southern officeholders might bring to light some elusive clues about the extent of change or continuity in Southern social psychology across the war years.

Comparative history has been in and out of vogue frequently. Comparing postwar settlements following the American Civil War with settlements after other more recent wars has not been received as very enlightening. Comparing the extent of change over a major war period, however, seems to me a useful way to isolate essentials. The Japanese and German experiences after the Second World War are only the most evident examples. One of my colleagues, interested in Japanese history, tells me that age cohort analysis seems very useful for this purpose. Youthful Japanese reared to regard the Emperor as divine may have suffered far greater trauma than older and more experienced Japanese upon hearing on radio the Emperor's own very ordinary voice denying his own divinity.[24] In the study of slave experience through the Federal Writers' Project Slave Narratives and other twentieth-century interview projects, Professor Paul Escott, as well as other users, is explicit in considering age of the respondent when slavery ended.[25] I think that there is nothing comparable in studying white responses to the war and its consequences, and sustained attention is needed to the well-established psychological dimensions of stages of development through the life cycle. Stage of development is sometimes strongly related to the outcome of grief from the loss of important persons, and one psychiatrist and biographer argues that such loss may "lay down a precipitate of character traits" and that this is "particularly true in children."[26] No other period in the American experience can match the extent of childhood bereavement among white Southerners during the Civil War. Where are the studies of the later behavior and influence of the age cohort that suffered this particular Civil War trauma? I certainly do not claim to know, but it may be more than coincidence that the children of the Civil War years were in their prime years for public leadership during the 1890s, when some significant things happened to the public forms of race relations in the South. Age cohort analysis, moreover, might help to answer a question posed during last night's discussion time. How did the idyllic antebellum slave image, Sambo and all, ever recover from the planters' wartime disenchantment with the attitudes and behavior of the black people? Again, I certainly do not know, but I think it may be worthwhile to try to identify the wartime ages of the principal contributors to the revived image. I am not unaware that some of the mature adults of wartime did later reminisce in that mode, perhaps sometimes for a contemporary practical purpose. It may well be, nonetheless, that it was the children of the Confederacy who could later actually believe the revived myth.

Numerical and formal analysis, partly encouraged by the development of computing machinery, has passed its bumptious stage and is settling down to be a modest but useful kind of history. It is my impression that, together with American Colonial history, partly Southern history, of course, the various periods and themes of Southern history have been receiving more than their fair share of sophisticated numerical analysis. Since much of this work has been inspired by growing concern with history from the bottom up, the South has been a fertile field to cultivate. For where in America, we may ask, can historians find a larger underprivileged element of society to study than in the nineteenth- and twentieth-century South? One of the most prolific segments of formal analysis, the New Economic History, has been devoted heavily to the South across the Civil War Era. The most persisting brouhaha in the profession in recent years stems from *Time on the Cross* and supplementing or challenging econometric studies of slavery and first freedom. So much of the New Economic History has been devoted to the South, in fact, that Harold D. Woodman recently provided a full-fledged historiographical essay on that growing body of work.[27]

Whether in the history of medicine, in the encouraging involvement of anthropologists and historical archaeologists with the history of the past century, or in the broadening facets of the more familiar intellectual history, the theme of our symposium this year provides both challenging and promising opportunities for the historians who will do the so-called new things ahead in the 1980s. The South Shall Rise Again was not written of Southern history; that has never fallen, and has never shown fewer signs of ever falling than it does right now.

Contributors

Thomas B. Alexander is professor of history at the University of Missouri at Columbia, and author of *Political Reconstruction in Tennessee* (1950), and, with Richard E. Beringer, *The Anatomy of the Confederate Congress* (1972).

Michael Barton is associate professor of history at the Pennsylvania State University, Capital Campus, and author of *Good-men: The Character of Civil War Soldiers* (1981).

Paul D. Escott is associate professor of history at the University of North Carolina at Charlotte, and author of *After Secession: Jefferson Davis and the Failure of Confederate Nationalism* (1978), and *Slavery Remembered: A Record of Twentieth Century Slave Narratives* (1979).

Leon F. Litwack is professor of history at the University of California at Berkeley, and author of *Been in the Storm So Long* (1980), which won the Pulitzer Prize in History in 1980.

Lawrence N. Powell is assistant professor of history at Tulane University, and author of *New Masters: Northern Planters during Civil War and Reconstruction* (1980).

Emory M. Thomas is professor of history at the University of Georgia, and author of *The Confederacy as a Revolutionary Experience* (1971), and *The Confederate Nation, 1861–1865* (1979).

Michael S. Wayne is assistant professor of history at the University of Toronto, and author of *The Reshaping of Plantation Society: The Natchez District, 1860–1880* (1982).

Notes

Notes to PREFACE

1. Emory M. Thomas, *The Confederate Nation* (Harper & Row, Publishers, 1979), xv, 299.

Notes to THE FAILURE OF CONFEDERATE NATIONALISM
by Paul D. Escott

1. William Morris, editor, *The American Heritage Dictionary of the English Language* (Boston: American Heritage Publishing Co., Inc. and Houghton Mifflin Company, 1969), p. 317.
2. Emory M. Thomas, *The Confederacy as a Revolutionary Experience* (Englewood Cliffs, N. J.: Prentice Hall, 1971).
3. Paul D. Escott, *After Secession: Jefferson Davis and the Failure of Confederate Nationalism* (Baton Rouge: Louisiana State University Press, 1978), chapters 3 and 5.
4. Professor Michael Holt recently summed up the view of the late Professor David Potter in these words: "Southern secession was not the result of a preexisting southern nationalism. The main impulse behind southern separatism was fear of the northern threat to slavery, not the kind of political unity based on cultural homogeneity and a widespread, self-conscious sense of a separate destiny that Potter defined as authentic nationalism." Michael F. Holt, "In Search of Southern Nationalism," *Reviews in American History*, Volume 8, Number 2 (June, 1980), p. 234. The author agrees with Potter.
5. Escott, *After Secession*, chapter 2.
6. Ibid., chapters 3–7.
7. Ibid., chapters 6–7 and p. 206. On the absence of consensus on war aims, see also Larry E. Nelson, *Bullets, Ballots, and Rhetoric* (Tuscaloosa: The University of Alabama Press, 1980).
8. See Thomas B. Alexander and Richard E. Beringer, *The Anatomy of the Confederate Congress* (Nashville: Vanderbilt University Press, 1972) and W. Buck Yearns, *The Confederate Congress* (Athens: University of Georgia Press, 1960).

9. Escott, *After Secession*, pp. 217–18; Bell Irvin Wiley, "Southern Reaction to Federal Invasion," *Journal of Southern History*, Vol. XVI (1950), pp. 491–510.

10. Gavin Wright, *The Political Economy of the Cotton South* (New York: W. W. Norton & Company, Inc., 1978), p. 35.

11. For an early example, see Edmund Morgan, *American Slavery, American Freedom* (New York: W. W. Norton & Company, Inc., 1975), pages 378–79. See also Mary Boykin Chestnut, *A Diary from Dixie*, edited by Ben Ames Williams, Sentry edition (Boston: Houghton Mifflin Company, 1949), p. 143.

12. Escott, *After Secession*, pp. 101, 28–29.

13. George M. Fredrickson, *The Black Image in the White Mind* (New York: Harper & Row, 1971); Eugene D. Genovese, "Yeoman Farmers in a Slaveholders' Democracy," *Agricultural History*, Volume 49 (April, 1975), pp. 331–42.

14. W. J. Cash, *The Mind of the South* (New York: Vintage Books, 1969, 1941), pp. 22–24, 38; Wright, *Political Economy*, pp. 39, 57–61, also 36. Forrest McDonald and Grady McWhiney have shown, in "The Antebellum Southern Herdsman: A Reinterpretation," *The Journal of Southern History*, Volume XLI, Number 2 (May, 1975), pp. 147–166, that livestock growers and drovers were a real, largely forgotten group in the South's economy. They do not estimate, however, what portion of the southern white population may have been embraced within this group. Their data show that many hogs were raised, that a small number of people devoted themselves exclusively to the production of livestock, and that a fair number of farmers may have fattened some hogs and raised extra corn for sale to the drovers. They have not shown a substantial dependence by yeomen upon the planters, and they describe circumstances of life for those in the livestock " 'industry' " that would do much to reinforce a yeoman's feeling of independence.

15. (United States Bureau of the Census), *The Statistical History of the United States* (New York: Basic Books, Inc., 1976), pp. 24–37.

The argument here is not that yeomen and planters were unaware of distinctions of status and class. Rather, the argument is that population density was so low, the daily lives of individuals so isolated, and the degree of personal independence so substantial that the realities of class intruded on people's lives relatively infrequently. In this respect the experience of antebellum southern yeomen was remarkably different from the experience of ordinary citizens today.

16. Clement Eaton, *The Mind of the Old South*, Revised Edition (Baton Rouge: Louisiana State University Press, 1967), pp. 147–50.

17. These are characteristics of the United States as well. American society in general has provided considerable scope for various self-interests and has not required much internal unity or cooperation. These may be basic qualities of the American social system.

18. Escott, *After Secession*, pp. 120, 116, 117, 119.

19. Ibid., pp. 121, 118, 117–19 and 144, 206. Beth G. Crabtree and James W. Patton, "*Journal of a Secesh Lady: The Diary of Catherine Ann Devereux Edmondston, 1860–1866* (Raleigh: Division of Archives and History, 1979), pp. 90, 195, 238, 241, 242, 263–64, 265–66, 270, 334, 284, 287.

20. Escott, *After Secession*, pp. 125, 132–34.

21. Ibid., chapters 3, 5, 7, and 9. See also James L. Roark, *Masters Without Slaves* (New York: W. W. Norton & Company, 1977), a masterful portrait of the planter class that agrees with the assessment given here.

22. See Roark, *Masters Without Slaves,* and Michael Perman, *Reunion Without Compromise* (New York: Cambridge University Press, 1973).

23. The best study of the Ku Klux Klan remains Allen W. Trelease's *White Terror* (New York: Harper & Row, 1971).

24. Joel Ashworth to Governor W. W. Holden, October 28, 1870, in U.S. Congress, *Senate Reports,* Forty-second Congress, First Session, Number 1, p. 64.

Notes to SELF-INTEREST AND THE DECLINE OF CONFEDERATE NATIONALISM
by Lawrence N. Powell and Michael S. Wayne

1. The essay is conveniently located in Potter's *The South and The Sectional Conflict* (Baton Rouge: Louisiana State University Press, 1968).

2. *Ibid.,* 54.

3. U. S. Grant to Brig. Genl. E. S. Dennis, July 11, 1863 (Typed copy in possession of Michael Wayne); Vol. VI, p. 30, in Duncan Papers, Department of Archives and Manuscripts, Louisiana State University [hereafter cited as LSU]; Tonie [Lovell] to Posie [Duncan],, December 1, 1861, in Quitman Family Papers, Southern Historical Collection, University of North Carolina, Chapel Hill [herefter cited as UNC].

4. Excellent surveys of these developments from different perspectives were recently published by two members of our symposium: Paul Escott. *After Secession: Jefferson Davis and the Failure of Confederate Nationalism* (Baton Rouge: Louisiana State University Press, 1978); and Emory M. Thomas, *The Confederate Nation, 1861–1865* (New York: Harper & Row, 1979).

5. Quoted in Bell I. Wiley, *The Road to Appomattox* (New York: Atheneum, 1968), 67.

6. James D. Waters to his mother, Feb. 12, 1864, Box 12, folder 5, Waters Family Papers, Essex Institute.

7. Excerpts from an old journal, Quitman Family Papers, UNC.

8. C. B. T[ompkins] to Mollie, March 1, 1863, in Tompkins Papers, Duke University. See also Lawrence N. Powell, *New Masters: Northern Planters during the Civil War and Reconstruction* (New Haven: Yale University Press, 1980), 8–24.

9. Quoted in Gabor S. Boritt, *Lincoln and the Economics of the American Dream* (Memphis: Memphis State University, 1978), 246–47.

10. Lorenzo Thomas to Edwin Stanton, Apr. 22, 1863, L. Thomas Letterbook, AGO-Generals Papers, National Archives [hereafter cited as NA].

11. Quoted in Charles N. Ramsdell, *Behind the Lines in the Southern Confederacy* (Baton Rouge: Louisiana State University Press, 1944), 110.

12. Quoted in Harold M. Hyman, *To Try Men's Souls: Loyalty Tests in American History* (Berkeley and Los Angeles: University of California Press, 1960), 174.

13. Boritt, *Lincoln and the American Dream,* 235–43; the quotation is on p. 243. See also Hyman, *To Try Men's Souls,* 167–97.

14. C. Peter Ripley, *Slaves and Freedmen in Civil War Louisiana* (Baton Rouge: Louisiana State University Press, 1976), 48–49; Louis Gerteis, *From Con-*

traband to Freedman: Federal Policy toward Southern Blacks, 1861–1865 (West-
port, Ct.: Greenwood Press, 1973); Roger W. Shugg, *Origins of Class Struggle in
Louisiana: A Social History of White Farmers and Laborers during Slavery and
After, 1840–1875* (Baton Rouge: Louisiana State University Press, 1967), 184;
Whitmore Diary (MS in UNC), September 22, 1863.

15. Bell Irvin Wiley, *Southern Negroes, 1861–1865* (New Haven: Yale University Press, 1965), 245.

16. Powell, *New Masters*, 3–4, 45, 181–82n; *The American Annual Cyclopaedia
. . . of the Year 1863* (New York, D. Appleton & Co., 1868), 428–29.

17. Stephen Duncan to General [James B.] McPherson, Dec. 14, 1863, filed
under John Heath Application in "Applications for Lease of Abandoned Plantations," Bureau of Refugees, Freedmen and Abandoned Lands, NA; Powell, *New
Masters*, 45.

18. Deposition by B. T. Montgomery, [1865], in Davis Papers, Mississippi
Department of Archives and History [hereafter cited as MA]; S[tephen], Duncan
to Dr. Wm. Harper, September 17, 1863, in Farrar papers, LSU.

19. R. A. Minor to William [Minor], March 10, 1864, in Minor Papers, LSU;
Fanny E. Conner to her husband, October 13, 1863, in Conner Papers, LSU.

20. Matilda Gresham, *Life of Walter Quintin Gresham, 1832–1895* (2 vols.;
Chicago: Rand McNally, 1919), I, 257n.

21. Kate Aubrey to Charlie, February [?], 1864, in Conner Papers, LSU.

22. See, for example, Foster Diary (MS in Duke University).

23. Henry C. Minor to father, Mar. 23, 1864, William J.Minor and Family
Papers, LSU.

24. Louisie [Lovell] to Capt. Joseph Lovell, February 24, 1864, [Louisa Quitman Lovell] to Capt. Joseph Lovell, July 29, 1864 L[ouisa Quitman Lovell] to
Posie [Duncan], April 8, 1865, all in Quitman Family Papers, UNC.

25. Quoted in David M. Potter, "Jefferson Davis and the Political Factors in
Confederate Defeat," in Potter, ed., *The South and the Sectional Conflict*, 269.

26. Quoted in Boritt, *Lincoln and the American Dream*, 244.

27. The best treatments of this subject are E. Merton Coulter, "Commercial
Intercourse with the Confederacy in the Mississippi Valley, 1861–1865," *Missis-
sippi Valley Historical Review*, 5 (Mar. 1919) 377–95; and Ludwell H. Johnson,
"Contraband Trade during the Last Year of the Civil War," in ibid., 49
(Mar.1963), 635–51.

28. John D. Winters, *The Civil War in Louisiana* (Baton Rouge: Louisiana
State University, 1963), 309; Ramsdell, *Behind the Lines*, 57–59, 107–08;
John K. Bettersworth, *Confederate Mississippi: The People and Policies of a
Cotton State in Wartime* (Baton Rouge: Louisiana State University Press, 1943),
203, 242–43, 249; Coulter, "Commerce with the Confederacy," 386–87; *DeBow's
Review*, After the War Series, 4 (Sept. 1867) 236.

29. Regarding the issue of "rent," see Shoemaker Diary (MS in Duke University), Mar. 24, 1864; see also Ramsdell, *Behind the Lines*, 106; Winters, *Civil War
in Louisiana*, 303–04, 309, 311, 323–24.

30. Ludwell H. Johnson, "Trading with the Union: The Evolution of Confederate Policy," *The Virginia Magazine of History and Biography*, 78 (July 1970),
308–25; Ramsdell, *Behind the Lines*, 110–11.

31. Notice of permission, undated, in Trask-Ventress Family Papers, MA.

32. Winters, *Civil War in Louisiana*, 406; Johnson, "Contraband Trade," 646–
52.

33. F. Y. C[arlile] to John C. Pedrick, Dec. 11, 1863, in Pedrick Papers, Duke.

34. Quoted in Coulter, "Commercial Intercourse," 393–94; Johnson, "Northern Profits and Profiteers; The Cotton Rings of 1864–1865," *Civil War History*, 12 (June 1966), 101–15.
35. Quoted in Boritt, *Lincoln and the American Dream*, 248.
36. Hattie to her brother, November 25, 1864, in Douglas Papers, UNC.
37. Chas. Whitmore to Mary Anne Welsh, November 25, 1863 (copy), in Whitmore Diary (MS in UNC).
38. Whitelaw Reid, *After the War: A Southern Tour* (Cincinnati: Moore, Wilstach & Baldwin, 1866), 485.
39. Joshua James to Major Genl. McClernand, April 27, 1863, [Joshua James] to Hon. Robert J. Walker, January 13, 1868 (unfinished copy), both in James Papers, Duke.
40. [Haller Nutt] to Honl. Reverdy Johnson, October [?], 1863 (microfilm copy from Huntington Library), in Nutt Papers, Duke.
41. Hyman, *To Try Men's Souls*, 196.
42. Powell, *New Masters*, 45; and Hyman, *To Try Men's Souls* 167–98, for a helpful survey of southern oath-taking during the war.
43. Gen. Thomas Kilby-Smith quoted in John Stanford Coussons, "The Federal Occupation of Natchez Mississippi, 1863–1865" (M.A. thesis, Louisiana State University, 1958), 100.
44. Receipts, November 20, 26, 27, 1863, all in Mercer Papers, LSU; see also, agreement, May 2, 1863, in Duncan Papers, LSU.
45. Memoranda of agreement, September 4, 16, 25, 30, all in Trask-Ventress Family Papers, MA.
46. Quoted in Powell, *New Masters*, 47.
47. Bettersworth, *Confederate Mississippi*, 151, 201; Winters, *Civil War* in Louisiana, 309. Charles Ramsdell is perceptive here: "Those who profited from this clandestine trade understood that, since it was only the Confederate laws they were violating, punishment was to be expected only from Confederate authority. They would, therefore, do nothing to increase that authority or restore it. They also realized that the relief or profits which the trade brought them would come to an end if the Federal armies should be driven away. This, at least, seems to have been the reaction of most of them—and this in a section where less than two years before the secession movement had been supported overwhelmingly." *Behind the Lines*, 59–60.
48. Lillian A. Pereyra, *James Lusk Alcorn: Persistent Whig* (Baton Rouge: Louisiana State University Press, 1966), 60–67.
49. D. B. Nailer to President Davis, Mar 11, 1864, Davis Papers, Duke.
50. Pereyra, *Alcorn*, 70.
51. Quoted in Bettersworth, *Confederate Mississippi*, 187.
52. James L. Roark, *Masters without Slaves, Southern Planters in the Civil War and Reconstruction* (New York: W. W. Norton & Company, 1977), 45.

Notes to DID THE CONFEDERACY CHANGE SOUTHERN SOLDIERS?
by MICHAEL BARTON

1. See Emory M. Thomas, *The Confederacy as a Revolutionary Experience* (Englewood Cliffs, N.J.: Prentice-Hall 1971) pp. 101, 117–118, 131–132; and Thomas, *The Confederate Nation: 1861–1865* (New York: Harper and Row, 1979), pp. 221, 224–225.

2. Michael Barton, *Goodmen: The Character of Civil War Soldiers* (University Park, Pa.: Pennsylvania State University Press, 1981) especially Chapter One. This essay is not part of the book.

3. William James, *Letters*, Vol. I (Boston: Atlantic Monthly Press, 1920), p. 199; cited in Erik Erikson, *Identity; Youth and Crisis* (New York: W. W. Norton, 1968), p. 19.

4. See Bruno Bettelheim, *Surviving and Other Essays* (New York: Knopf, 1979).

5. Kenneth Gergen, "The Decline of Character: Socialization and Self-Consistency," in Gordon J. DiRenzo, ed. *We, The People: American Character and Social Change* (Westport, Conn.: Greenwood Press, 1977), pp. 255–272.

6. On this general matter, see Erving Goffman, *The Presentation of Self in Everyday Life*(Garden City, N.Y.: Anchor Books ed., 1959).

7. The main "scientific" studies of personal documents are Gordon W. Allport, *The Use of Personal Documents in Psychological Science* (New York: Social Science Research Council Bulletin 49, 1942), and Louis Gottschalk, Clyde Kluckhohn, and Robert Angell, *The Use of Personal Documents in History, Anthropology, and Sociology* (New York: Social Science Research Council Bulletin 53, 1945). See also Michael Barton, "The Character of Civil War Soldiers: A Comparative Analysis of the Language of Moral Evaluation in Diaries" (Ph.D. Diss., Univ. of Pennsylvania, 1974), Chs. 2–4.

8. See Murray Murphey, *Our Knowledge of the Historical Past* (Indianapolis: Bobbs-Merrill, 1973), for a critique of conventional historical narrative, logic, and interpretation.

9. "Unobtrusive," in the sense I use it here, comes from Eugene J. Webb, Donald T. Campbell, Richard D. Schwartz, and Lee Sechrest, *Unobtrusive Measures: Nonreactive Research in the Social Sciences* (Chicago: Rand-McNally, 1966). They use it to mean evidence which is "subtle" and "not obvious" to the researchers as well as to the subjects. "Unobtrusive measures" are revealing "oddball" clues left behind by subject who might otherwise have reacted and changed their behavior if they were observed and studied directly.

10. See Barton, *Goodmen*, Appendix I.

11. See Barton, *Goodmen*, pp. 28–29, 53–54.

12. See Barton, *Goodmen*, pp. 45–46.

13. R. Brown and A. Gilman, "The Pronouns of Power and Solidarity," in T. Sebeok, *Style in Language* (New York: Wiley, 1960).

Sources

Southern Officers

Alison, Joseph Dill. "War Diary of Dr. Joseph Dill Alison of Carlowville, Alabama." *Alabama Historical Quarterly*, 9 (1947), 385–98.

Bedford, A. M. "Diary Kept by Capt. A. M. Bedford, Third Missouri Cavalry, while on Morris Island, S. C., Prisoner of War at Hilton Head and Fort Pulaski." In *The Immortal Six Hundred*. John O. Murray. n.p., 1911, pp. 250–319.

Brown, John Henry. "'The Paths of Glory' (The War-time Diary of Maj. John Henry Brown, C.S.A.)." Ed. W. J. Lemke. *Arkansas Historical Quarterly*, 15 (1956), 344–59.

Cooke, Giles Buckner. "Rev.-Maj. Giles Buckner Cooke. [Diary Excerpts]" *Tyler's Quarterly*, 19 (1937–38), 1–10, 87–94.

Cox, Abner R. "South From Appomattox: The Diary of Abner R. Cox." Ed. Royce Gordon Shingleton. *South Carolina Historical Magazine*, 75 (1974), 238–44.

Craig, J. M. "The Diary of Surgeon Craig, Fourth Louisiana Regiment, C.S.A., 1864–65." John S. Kendall. *Louisiana Historical Quarterly*, 8 (1925), 53–70.

Douglas, James P. "Diary of James P. Douglas, 1864." In *Douglas's Texas Battery*. Ed. Lucia Rutherford Douglas. Tyler, Texas: Smith County Historical Society, 1966, pp. 202–214.

Fleming, Robert H. "The Confederate Naval Cadets and the Confederate Treasure: The Diary of Midshipman Robert H. Fleming." Ed. G. Melvin Herndon. *Georgia Historical Quarterly*, 50 (1966), 207–16.

Fullam, George Townley. *The Journal of George Townley Fullam, Boarding Officer of the Confederate Sea Raider Alabama*. Ed. Charles G. Summersell. University, Ala.: University of Alabama Press, 1973.

Gailor, Frank M. "The Diary of a Confederate Quartermaster." Eds. Charlotte Cleveland and Robert Daniel. *Tennessee Historical Quarterly*, 11 (1952), 78–85.

Garnett, James Mercer. "Diary of Captain James M. Garnett, Ordnance Officer of Rodes's Division, 2d Corps, Army of Northern Virginia, From August 5th to November 30th, 1864, covering part of General Early's Campaign in the Shenandoah Valley." *Southern Historical Society Papers*, 27 (1899), 1–16; 28 (1900), 58–71.

Gorgas, Josiah. *The Civil War Diary of General Josiah Gorgas*. Ed. Frank E. Vandiver. University, Ala.: University of Alabama Press. 1947.

Gray, Richard L. "Prison Diary of Lieutenant Richard L. Gray." In *Diaries, Letters, and Recollections of the War Between the States*. Winchester-Frederick County Historical Society Papers, Winchester, Virginia. Vol. 3, 1955, pp.30–45.

Hall, James E. *The Diary of a Confederate Soldier, James E. Hall*. Ed. Ruth Woods Dayton. Charleston, W. Va.: privately printed, 1961.

Harris, John H. "Diary of Captain John H. Harris." In *Confederate Stamps, Old Letters, and History*. Raynor Hubbel. Privately printed, 1959, pp. 2–13.

Hinson, William G. "The Diary of William G. Hinson During the War of Secession." Ed. Joseph Ioor Waring. *South Carolina Historical Magazine*, 75 (1974), 14–23, 111–20.

Hotchkiss, Jedediah. *Make Me a Map of the Valley; The Civil War Journal of Stonewall Jackson's Topographer*. Ed. Archie P. McDonald. Dallas: Southern Methodist University Press, 1973.

Key Thomas J. *Two Soldiers; The Campaign Diaries of Thomas J. Key, C.S.A., December 7, 1863–May 17, 1865, and Robert J. Campbell, U.S.A., January 1, 1864–July 21, 1864*. Ed. Wirt Armistead Cate. Chapel Hill: University of North Carolina Press, 1938.

Killgore, Gabriel M. "Vicksburg Diary: The Journal of Gabriel M. Killgore." Ed. Douglas Maynard. *Civil War History*, 10 (1964), 33–53.

Little, Henry. "The Diary of General Henry Little, C.S.A." Ed. Albert Castel. *Civil War Times Illustrated*, 11 (October, 1972), 4–11, 41–7.

Luria, Albert Moses. "Albert Moses Luria, Gallant Young Confederate." *American Jewish Archives*, 7 (1955), 90–103.

McCreary, James Bennett. "The Journal of My Soldier Life." Contribs. Robert N.

McCreary and Mrs. Gatewood Gay. *Register of the Kentucky Historical Society*, 33 (1935), 97–117, 191–211.

McGavock, Randal W. *Pen and Sword: The Life and Journals of Randal W. McGavock, Colonel, C.S.A.* Ed. Jack Allen. Nashville: Tennessee Historical Commission, 1959.

Minor, Hubbard Taylor, Jr. "'I am Getting a Good Education . . .': An Unpublished Diary by a Cadet at the Confederate Naval Academy." *Civil War Times Illustrated*. 13 (November, 1974), 25–32; "Diary of a Confederate Naval Cadet: Conclusion." *Civil War Times Illustrated*, 13 (December, 1974), 24–36.

O'Brien, George W. "The Diary of Captain George W. O'Brien, 1863." Ed. Cooper W. Ragan. *Southwestern Historical Quarterly*, 67 (1963), 26–54, 235–46, 413–33.

Page, Richard C. M. "Diary of Major R. C. M. Page, Chief of Confederate States Artillery, Department of Southwest Virginia and East Tennessee, from October, 1864, to May, 1865." *Southern Historical Society Papers*, 16 (1888), 58–68.

Park, Robert Emory. "War Diary of Capt. Robert Emory Park, Twelfth Alabama Regiment, January 28th, 1863-January 27th, 1864. Accounts of the Battles of Chancellorsville, Gettysburg, Jeffersonton, Bristow Station, Locust Grove, Mine Run, the March into Maryland and Pennsylvania, with Reminiscences of the Battle of Seven Pines." *Southern Historical Society Paper*, 26 (1898), 1–31.

Pendleton, William Frederic. *Confederate Diary: Capt. W. F. Pendleton, January to April, 1865*. Bryn Athyn, Pa.: privately printed, 1957.

Pressley, John G. "Extracts from the Diary of Lieutenant-Colonel John G. Pressley, of the Twenty-fifth South Carolina Volunteers." *Southern Historical Society Papers*, 14 (1886), 35–62.

Semmes, Raphael. "Admiral on Horseback: The Diary of Brigadier General Raphael Semmes, February–May, 1865." Ed. W. Stanley Hoole. *Alabama Review*, 28 (1975), 12–50.

Sheeran, James B. *Confederate Chaplain: A War Journal of Rev. James B. Sheeran, 14th Louisiana, C.S.A.* Ed. Rev. Joseph T. Durkin. Milwaukee: Bruce Publishing Co., 1960.

Smith, Isaac Noyes. "A Virginian's Dilemma (The Civil War diary of Isaac Noyes Smith in which he describes the activities of the 22nd Regiment of Virginia Volunteers, Sept. to Nov., 1861)." Ed. William C. Childers. *West Virginia History*, 27 (1966), 173–200.

Speer, William H. A. "A Confederate Soldier's View of Johnson's Island Prison." Ed. James B. Murphy. *Ohio History*, 79 (1970), 101–1.

Steele, Nimrod Hunter. "The Nimrod Hunter Steele Diary and Letters." In *Diaries, Letters, and Recollections of the War Between the States*. Winchester-Frederick County Historical Society Papers, Winchester, Virginia Vol. 3, 1955, pp. 48–57.

Stevenson, William Grafton. "Diary of William Grafton Stevenson, Captain, C.S.A." Ed. Carl Rush Stevenson. *Alabama Historical Quarterly*, 23 (1961), 45–72.

Taylor, Thomas J. "'An Extraordinary Perseverance,' The Journal of Capt. Thomas J. Taylor, C.S.A." Eds. Lillian Taylor Wall and Robert M. McBride. *Tennessee Historical Quarterly*, 31 (1972), 328–59.

Trimble, Isaac Ridgeway. "The Civil War Diary of General Isaac Ridgeway Trimble." Ed. William Starr Myers. *Maryland Historical Magazine*, 17 (1922), 1–20.

Vaughan, Turner. "Diary of Turner Vaughan, Co. 'C.' 4th Alabama Regiment, C.S.A., Commenced March 4th, 1863 and Ending February 12th, 1864." *Alabama Historical Quarterly*, 18 (1956) 573–604.

Wescoat, Joseph Julius. "Diary of Captain Joseph Julius Wescoat, 1863–1865." Ed. Anne King Gregorie. *South Carolina Historical Magazine*, 59 (1958), 11–23, 84–95.

Womack, James J. *The Civil War Diary of Capt. J. J. Womack, Co. E, Sixteenth Regiment, Tennessee Volunteers, (Confederate).* McMinnville, Tenn.: Womack Printing Co., 1961.

Woolwine, Rufus James. "The Civil War Diary of Rufus J. Woolwine." Ed. Louis H. Manarin. *Virginia Magazine of History and Biography*, 71 (1963), 416–48.

Wright, Marcus Joseph. "Diary of Brigadier-General Marcus Joseph Wright, C.S.A., from April 23, 1861, to February 26, 1863." *William and Mary College Quarterly*, 2nd Ser., 15 (1935), 89–95.

Southern Enlisted

Andrews, W. H. *Diary of W. H. Andrews, 1st Sergt. Co. M, 1st Georgia Regulars, from Feb. 1861, to May 2, 1865.* East Atlanta: n.p., 1891?

Barrow, Willie Micajah. "The Civil War diary of Willie Micajah Barrow, September 23, 1861–July 13, 1862." Eds. Wendell H. Stephenson and Edwin A. Davis. *Louisiana Historical Quarterly*, 17 (1934), 436–51, 712–31.

Chambers, William Pitt. "My Journal, 1862." *Publications of the Mississippi Hisorical Society*, NS, 5 (1925), 221–386.

Clement, Abram Wilson. "Diary of Abram W. Clement, 1865." Ed. Slann L. C. Simmons. *South Carolina Historical Magazine*, 59 (1958), 78–83.

Dodd, Ephraim Shelby. *Diary of Ephraim Shelby Dodd, Member of Company D, Terry's Texas Rangers, December 4, 1862–January 1, 1864.* Austin, Texas: Press of E. L. Steck, 1914.

Dodd, James M. "Civil War Diary of James M. Dodd of the 'Cooper Guards.'" *Register of the Kentucky Historical Society*, 59 (1961), 343–9.

Fauntleroy, James Henry. "Elkhorn to Vicksburg [James H. Fauntleroy's Diary for the Year 1862]" Homer L. Calkin. *Civil War History*, 2 (1956), 7–43.

Hamilton, James Allen. "The Civil War Diary of James Allen Hamilton, 1861–1864." Ed. Alwyn Barr. *Texana*, 2 (1964), 132–45.

Haney, John H. "Bragg's Kentucky Campaign: A Confederate Soldier's Account." Eds. Will Frank Steely and Orville W. Taylor. *Register of the Kentucky Historical Society*, 57 (1959), 49–55.

Haynes, Draughton Stith. *The Field Diary of a Confederate Soldier, Draughton Stith Haynes, While Serving With the Army of Northern Virginia, C.S.A.* Darien, Ga.: Ashantilly Press, 1963.

Heartsill, William Williston. *Fourteen Hundred and Ninety-One Days in the Confederate Army.* 1876; rpt. Jackson, Tenn.: McCowat-Mercer Press, 1954, pp. 269–92.

Holmes, Robert Masten. *Kemper County Rebel: The Civil War Diary of Robert*

Masten Holmes, C.S.A. Ed. Frank Allen Dennis. Jackson: University and College Press of Mississippi, 1973.

Jones, John B. *A Rebel War Clerk's Diary at the Confederate States Capital.* Vol. 1. Ed. Howard Swiggett. New York: Old Hickory Bookshop, 1935.

Kean, Robert Garlick Hill. *Inside the Confederate Government: The Diary of Robert Garlick Hill Kean.* Ed. Edward Younger. New York: Oxford University Press, 1957, pp. 3–27.

Law, John G. "Diary of a Confederate Soldier." Rev. J. G. Law. *Southern Historical Society Papers,* 10 (1882), 378–81, 564–9; 11 (1883), 175–81, 297–303, 460–5; 12 (1884), 22–8, 215–9, 390–5, 538–43.

Leon, Louis. *Diary of a Tar Heel Confederate Soldier.* Charlotte, North Carolina: Stone Publishing Co., 1913.

Malone, Bartlett Yancey. *Whipt 'em Everytime: The Diary of Bartlett Yancey Malone, Co. H 6th N.C. Regiment.* Ed. William Whatley Pierson, Jr. Jackson, Tenn.: McCowat-Mercer Press, 1960.

Medford, Harvey C. "The Diary of H. C. Medford, Confederate Soldier, 1864." Eds. Rebecca W. Smith and Marion Mullins. *Southwestern Historical Quarterly,* 34 (1930), 106–40, 203–30.

Moore, Robert Augustus. *A Life for the Confederacy, as Recorded in the Pocket Diaries of Pvt. Robert A. Moore, Co. G, 17th Mississippi Regiment Confederate Guards, Holly Springs, Mississippi:* Ed. James W. Silver. Jackson, Tenn.: McCowat-Mercer Press, 1959.

Morgan, George P. "A Confederate Journal." Ed. George E. Moore. *West Virginia History,* 22 (1961), 201–6.

Morgan, Stephen A. "A Confederate Journal." Ed. George E. Moore. *West Virginia History,* 22 (1961), 207–16.

Nixon, Liberty Independence. "An Alabamian at Shiloh: The Diary of Liberty Independence Nixon." Ed. Hugh C. Bailey. *Alabama Review,* 11 (1958), 144–55.

Patrick, Robert Draughton. *Reluctant Rebel: The Secret Diary of Robert Patrick, 1861–1865.* Ed. F. Jay Taylor. Baton Rouge: Louisiana State University Press, 1959.

Patterson, Edmund DeWitt. *Yankee Rebel: The Civil War Journal of Edmund DeWitt Patterson.* Ed. John G. Barnett. Chapel Hill: University of North Carolina Press, 1966.

Porter, William Clendenin. "War Diary of W. C. Porter." Ed. J. V. Frederick. *Arkansas Historical Quarterly,* 11 (1952), 286–314.

Seaton, Benjamin M. *The Bugle Softly Blows: The Confederate Diary of Benjamin M. Seaton.* Ed. Col. Harold B. Simpson. Waco: Texian Press, 1965.

Smith, James West. "A Confederate Soldier's Diary: Vicksburg in 1863." *Southwest Review,* 28 (1943), 293–327.

Smith, Thomas Crutcher. *Here's Yer Mule: The Diary of Thomas C. Smith, 3rd Sergeant, Company 'G,' Wood's Regiment, 32nd Texas Cavalry, C.S.A., March 30, 1862–December 31,1862.* Waco: Little Texian Press, 1958.

Townsend, Harry C. "Townsend's Diary —January–May, 1965. From Petersburg to Appomattox, Thence to North Carolina to Join Johnston's Army." *Southern Historical Society Papers,* 34 (1906), 99–127.

Williamson, John Coffee. "The Civil War Diary of John Coffee Williamson." Ed. J. C. Williamson. *Tennessee Historical Quarterly,* 15 (1956), 61–74.

Notes to THE DIMENSIONS OF CONTINUITY ACROSS THE CIVIL WAR
by Thomas B. Alexander

1. *Journal of Southern History*, XXX (November, 1964), 451–62.
2. *Journal of Interdisciplinary History*, XII (Summer and Autumn, 1981). Peter H. Smith's essay is in the Summer issue, pp. 3–27.
3. Sidney Andrews, *The South Since the War* (Boston, 1866),135–36.
4. Thomas B. Alexander, "Persistent Whiggery in the Confederate South, 1860–1877," *Journal of Southern History*, XXVII (August, 1961), 305–29.
5. Earlene Williams Collier, "Response of Southern Editors and Political Leaders to the National Union Convention Movement of 1866" (M.A. thesis, University of Alabama, 1963).
6. William C. Harris, *Presidential Reconstruction in Mississippi* (Baton Rouge: Louisiana State University Press, 1967);*ibid.,The Day of the Carpetbagger: Republican Reconstruction in Mississippi* (Baton Rouge and London; Louisiana State University Press, 1979); William McKinley Cash, "Alabama Republicans During Reconstruction: Personal Characteristics, Motivations, and Political Activity of Party Activists, 1867–1880" (Ph.D. dissertation, University of Alabama, 1973).
7. Jonathan M. Wiener, *Social Origins of the New South: Alabama, 1860–1885* (Baton Rouge and London: Louisiana State University Press, 1978).
8. J. Carlyle Sitterson, "Business Leaders in Post-Civil War North Carolina, 1865–1900," in *Studies in Southern History in Memory of Albert Ray Newsome, 1894–1951* (Chapel Hill: University of North Carolina Press,1957).
9. Marjorie Howell Cook [now Mrs. Krebs], "Restoration and Innovation: Alabamians Adjust To Defeat, 1865–1867" (Ph.D. dissertation, University of Alabama, 1968).
10. Westley Floyd Busbee, Jr., "Presidential Reconstruction in Georgia, 1865–1867" (Ph.D. dissertation, University of Alabama, 1972).
11. Cash, "Alabama Republicans During Reconstruction."
12. Vicki L. Vaughn, "Southern Commercial Conventions: Continuity of Perceptions, Values, and Leadership, 1837–1871" (Ph.D. dissertation, University of Missouri—Columbia, 1979).
13. *Journal of Southern History*, XV (February, 1949), 3–8.
14. Harris, *Day of the Carpetbagger;* Joe Gray Taylor, *Louisiana Reconstructed, 1863–1877* (Baton Rouge and London: Louisiana State University Press, 1974).
15. University Press of Kentucky, 1975.
16 *Journal of Southern History*, XLVIII (February 1982).
17. Furnished by Dr. Susan C. Boyle from an ongoing project under the direction of Professor Susan L. Flader of the University of Missouri—Columbia.
18. Leon F. Litwack, *Been in the Storm So Long* (New York: Alfred A. Knopf, 1979).
19. Roark, *Masters Without Slaves: Southern Planters in the Civil War and Reconstruction* (New York: W. W. Norton & Company, 1977).
20. *American Historical Review*, Volume 85 (December 1980), 1095–1118.
21. Gavin Wright, *The Political Economy of the Cotton South: Households, Markets, and Wealth in the Nineteenth Century* (New York: W. W. Norton & Company, 1978).

22. Michael Barton, *Goodmen: The Character of Civil War Soldiers* (University Park and London: Pennsylvania State University Press, 1981).

23. Ph.D. dissertation, University of Alabama, 1972.

24. I am endebted to Professor Robert M. Somers for this insight.

25. Paul D. Escott, *Slavery Remembered: A Record of Twentieth-Century Slave Narratives* (Chapel Hill: University of North Carolina Press, 1979).

26. Miles F. Shore, "Biography in the 1980s: A Psychoanalytic Perspective," *Journal of Interdisciplinary History*, XII (Summer, 1981), 89–113.

27. Woodman, "Sequel to Slavery: The New History Views the Postbellum South," *Journal of Southern History*, XLIII (November 1977), 523–54.